Implementing an Analytics Culture for Data Driven Decisions

Robert James Zwerling

Jesper Hybholt Sorensen

CONTENTS

ACKNOWLEDGMENTS

We thank our wives for being persistent getting our thoughts down on paper and supporting us throughout the writing of this book.

Also, thanks to the people who have taken time to give us constructive feedback to the content of the book.

Finally, this book expresses our vision for the advancement of Finance to take a leadership role in performance improvement through data driven decisions from analytics.

Implementing an Analytics Culture for Data Driven Decisions

1 INTRODUCTION

Nothing is more terrible than activity without insight – Thomas Carlyle[1]

For ages Finance held the role of the trusted scorekeeper; closing the books, complying with rules and regulation, and monitoring company financial performance to assure the company delivers on its targets and strategy. Focus has been on looking at historical data and, at best, comparing it with a budget prepared once a year, which quickly got outdated. Technology was, and remains, spreadsheets as the primary tool for analysis, reporting, and planning.

In recent years this has been changing as uncertainty has increased and the amount of data available to companies has grown to unimaginable amounts. Someone needs to make sense of it all yet, while many including Finance have been trying hard, few have managed to do so. This has got to change, and we see Finance taking a lead role in building a *culture* of data driven decisions using advanced analytics. This book explains how.

Without Insight you have nothing

First, it's important to understand that while you can analyze as much as you want on the vast amounts of data, it is worth nothing without deriving insights from it. Insight is that which you don't know and if known will influence the decision that will be made. Further, insights must be clear, understandable, and discussable with business stakeholders. This has been the Achilles Heel of Finance.

Up until now Finance analyzed and analyzed in large spreadsheets and BI tools but was unable to provide true insights. Finance simply recorded WHAT happened. That was obvious to the business stakeholders themselves and, while they liked the waterfall chart and first-level explanations, they needed no more. An e-mail would do for any future interactions. To have a seat-at-the-table, Finance needs a strategy and, in our opinion, it's simple.

1. Explaining WHAT happened allows you to send the e-mail
2. Explaining WHERE it happened makes people open your e-mail

3. Explaining WHY it happened gets you a meeting with the business leaders
4. Predicting WHAT MIGHT happen if changes are not made gets you a seat at the table
5. Predicting HOW TO MAKE IT happen gets the business to always take decisions with Finance

While this seems simple it has proven hard for Finance, in general, to crack the code on how to do this effectively. Finance just has been sending e-mails (and reports generated on stakeholder's requests) without following through on their effect.

The sad fact is that many of the activities done in Finance today could be stopped tomorrow and no one would feel the difference. Things must be done differently, and it starts with developing insights as to WHY something happened. Without those insights we should drastically reduce the size of Finance.

Deliver Insight means building an Analytics Culture

Finance has to transform from being unconsciously analytically incompetent to unconsciously analytically competent, and it's going to be a journey. The good news is the journey does not have to be hard, long, or expensive. It need only be disciplined.

We will learn how to align and institutionalize the process of analytics that will lead to building a culture in Finance of data driven decisions.

It's not that Finance lacks information, but rather that Finance needs structure and tools to analyze in a way that yields insights and foresight to facilitate a dialogue with stakeholders. That dialogue will reveal unseen opportunities for gain and unknown corridors of risks. The result will be better decisions that lead to growth that is a plan vs. being a reed-in-the-wind of the market.

The path to an Analytics Culture

This book develops the Roadmap to a culture of data driven decisions from analytics to create sustainable business performance improvement. It will transform Finance into a world class strategic partner with the business. It will develop the four components of building the analytics culture of Mindset, People, Processes, and Systems.

We will start with a discussion of Next Generation Finance, layout the Roadmap of an analytics culture, and give the framework for benchmarking your journey in creating the analytics culture and its impact on business performance. Next, we'll explore each component of the analytics culture. Then, offer skills for storytelling with analytics to assure analytics can be absorbed into the decision-making process. Finally, we'll landscape how to "sell" a culture of analytics to Finance and the business.

Why we do Analytics

The pot-of-gold for successfully implementing a culture of data driven decisions through analytics is, well, a pot-of-gold! Our research of public companies shows that those companies that continuously deliver reliable revenue and earnings growth are rewarded, on average, with a forward PE multiple 27% higher than the average PE multiple of a comparable market basket of companies.

Further, there is a "human" component – that of career betterment and job satisfaction. Let's face it, there are many high IQ people in Finance that spend the bulk of their day in cut/paste into spreadsheets. Using analytics makes one more valuable to the business and delivering insights from those analytics gives one a heightened sense of worth and accomplishment.

2 NEXT GENERATION FINANCE

Science is the process that takes us from confusion to understanding in a manner that's precise, predictive and reliable - a transformation, for those lucky enough to experience it, that is empowering – Brian Greene[1]

Finance has the core functions as the "Controller" and "specialist". The former is focused on compliance, governance, reporting to the external market, corporate finance, and Investor Relations. Some level of communication skill is needed for reporting to the CEO office and to the external market. The specialist includes BI, Consolidation, Internal Audit, Treasury, and Tax.

These core functions have particular technical skills and influence high level company decisions but have limited influence on day to day operational decisions. As depicted on Figure 2-1 below, the other Finance function is the "Trusted Scorekeeper". However, the modern CFO envisions Finance advancing to the "Strategic Partner" to the business.

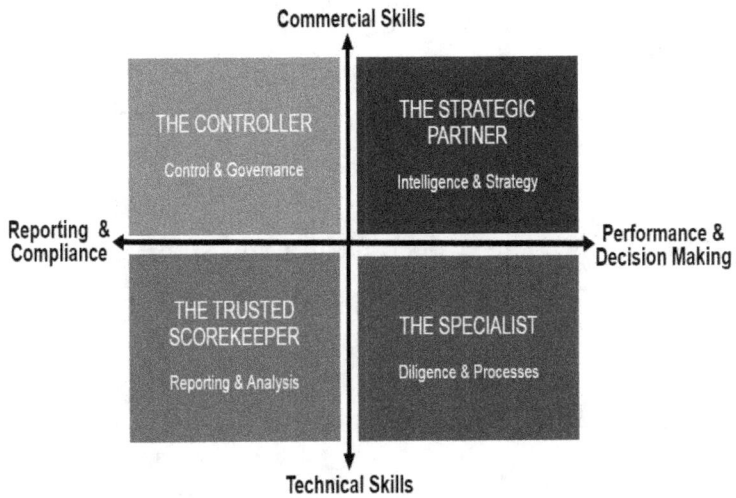

Figure 2.1: The Roles of Finance

Until very recently, the role of Finance has been focused on trusted scorekeeping including reporting historical numbers and providing variance explanations to business partners. The role has, to a large extent, been focused on telling what has happened against the budget, last year, and the forecast. For decades that has been enough for Finance to have a seat at the table, but after the millennium a change in the role of Finance began.

For Finance to have a seat at the table in today's business it is no longer enough just to print reports and do analysis on historical information. Modern Finance builds business skills, speaks the business language, and understands the business to provide better storytelling of financial performance.

With recent emergent technologies and a change in mentality of wanting to influence decisions, Finance has started the journey of advancing from the Trusted Scorekeeper towards the Strategic Partner. The latter transforms Finance into a catalyst that engages analytics intelligence to deliver deep insight and strategic foresight to empower data driven decisions.

The Journey Starts with Efficiencies

Advancing the analytical skillset cannot be an additional cost to Finance, so as a prerequisite, it needs to change the way it operates.

The first wave of Finance Transformation, at the beginning of the 21st Century, was often focused on moving transaction related tasks to low cost locations. As we are getting closer to 2020, a lot of the traditional standard reporting has moved to control centers too. Both actions free resources in Finance to invest in skillsets that deliver more value-add insight and foresight through the use of analytics.

The use of more sophisticated tools beyond Excel also

provides Finance an ability to drive efficiencies. For example, Data Visualization tools enables Finance to be more efficient producing reporting and analysis.

With improved efficiencies, focus can be towards driving more value-add analytics, which enables business leaders to take better and faster decisions. The agility of Finance is crucial for its ability to play a continuous central role in business operations.

Next Generation Finance Transformation

For many years Finance has had a monopoly on reporting numbers to business leaders, but this monopoly no longer exists. In the digital world, data flows everywhere and Finance needs to collaborate and build relationships to gain access to some of that data. Further, larger companies are creating analytics centers that will "compete" with Finance to serve the business. In some instances, these centers will be the right place for analytics but, unless Finance gets into the analytics game, Finance risks being replaced in many of its FP&A functions.

Gaining access to data and turning it into insights for data driven decisions is crucial for, what we call, "Next Generation Finance". Here, Finance provides value added analysis that is more than just standard financial information. Further, Finance must build a relationship with and understanding of the operations of the business.

The combination of analytical insights and business collaboration is essential or there is a high risk of Finance getting side-lined.

Heretofore what was known as "Finance Transformation" projects (to be distinguished from what we propose as Next Generation Finance) have often failed because the desire to add value ends with expense focused initiatives. The result is a reduction in the number of Finance employees, since the focus is effectiveness and efficiencies. Finance ends-up as the cost cutter and not the enabler for top line growth.

Finance also struggles selling the concept of "Finance Transformation", especially, if its business partners have no appetite for data driven decisions and just want financial reporting on past performance.

According to Deloitte[2] only 8% of companies surveyed see Finance as the primary source of insight for decision making. To add insult-to-injury, the bastion of regular reporting that Finance provides has marginal value. For example, the National Retail Federation sites that "80% of reports never get used because they don't provide end users with the value they need out of them."

In companies that have little appetite for improvement (i.e. good enough is good enough) Finance Transformation will be impossible. However, for the rest, Finance can evolve to Next Generation Finance with leadership that understands the value of a culture of data driven decisions from analytics.

Achieving Next Generation Finance

Traditional Finance Transformation has the admirable focus on better and more efficient reporting, understanding how to communicate with executives, and building strong business acumen (i.e. operational knowledge of the business). Competencies like reporting & analysis, communicating with impact, understanding the business operation, and partnership building are the skillsets sought.

Next Generation Finance builds upon these skillsets with the addition to empower Finance to drive value added analytics that business leaders use to take data driven decisions.

Next Generation Finance is additive to cost cutting by expanding value to accelerate top line growth.

The most valuable CFO competency today is the knowledge of how to transform Finance from a hindsight looking spreadsheet driven accounting/reporting center to a value-add top line forward-looking predictive hub. Next Generation Finance follows the Figure 2-2 below, from traditional **Basics** and **Acumen** that builds to **Intelligence** and **Strategy**, with Intelligence the first step to an enabler for top line growth.

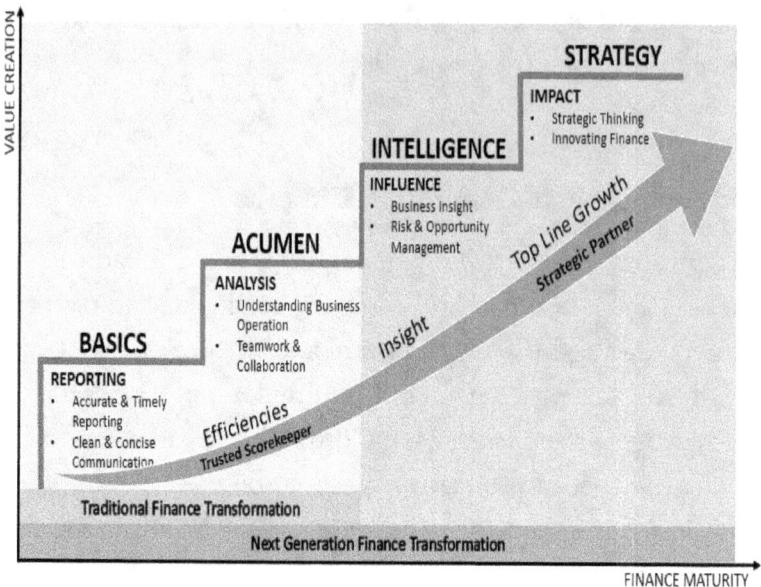

Figure 2-2: Next Generation Finance[3]

Intelligence is a deep understanding of the business value drivers and how to evaluate risk and opportunities. For example, according to studies by Oracle and CGMA[4] the most significant business value drivers are customer satisfaction, quality of business processes, customer relationship, quality of people, and brand reputation. Finance can bring analytics to quantify the relationship between value drivers and business performance to deliver insight not yet known by the business to enable better decisions.

The top-shelf of Next Generation Finance is Strategy that encompasses how Finance is positioned to impact the strategic direction of the company. Here, Finance establishes itself as an institution that is always consulted by business leaders before important decisions are made. Finance becomes the decision "glue" and has significant understanding of strategies to drive better decisions.

Finance innovates to predict future events and persuade business leaders to take data driven decisions based on analytical foresight. Finance, at this level, has access to advanced analytical tools and uses big data analytics to predict, in detail, events.

As Such, Next Generation Finance is about enabling Finance to master The Three *I's* . . . *Insight, Influence, and Impact.*

Analytics provides the __Insight__ to tell the business something it does not know, which __Influence__ their decisions, and __Impact__ the strategic direction of the company.

Evolution of Analytics

The "Evolution of Analytics" depicted on Figure 2-3 below, charts analytics stages and analytical techniques that have been available to Finance over the past 40 years. Advanced Finance organizations work across the full spectrum of Value Creation whereas immature organizations only work on the left side of the figure.

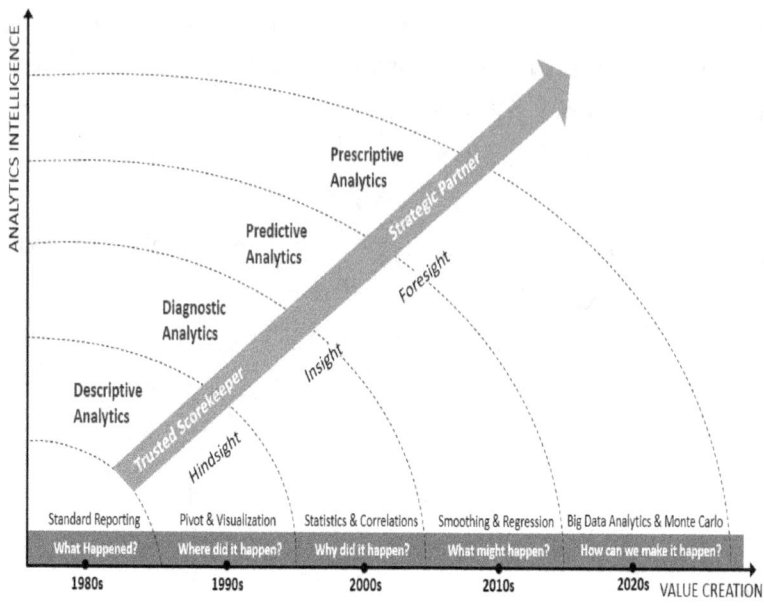

Figure 2-3: The Evolution of Analytics

There is a progression of analytics that begins with **Descriptive Analytics** that answers the question "Where did it happen?" and is characterized by the use of Business Intelligence (BI) and/or Excel to find variance in last year, budget, or the forecast. Descriptive Analytics also includes visualization using various charts to generate a narrative story.

As Finance gains maturity it adds **Diagnostic Analytics.** Here, data is examined to answer the question "Why did it happen?". It is characterized by analytical techniques, such as, data discovery, correlations, clusters and statistics that take a deeper look to attempt to understand the causes of change.

Here Finance has automated reporting to free time for true analytics. The focus has moved from providing hindsight information to generating insight. Use of simple statistics to provide correlations, mean, median, and standard deviation tell the business what the data means.

As Finance advances to **Predictive Analytics,** it establishes skills and uses advanced tools and techniques to generate value added foresight. Predictive Analytics is the practice of extracting information from existing data in order to ·reveal patterns that can predict future outcomes and trends.

With Predictive Analytics, Finance seeks foresight to answer, "What might happen?". Finance often experience that business leaders have their own opinion of future performance. However, this is typically built on a single case example, gut feeling, or simple historical comparisons. With Predictive Analytics, Finance can influence business leaders with an unbiased and scientific quantitative forecast.

Prescriptive Analytics answers the questions "How to make things happen?" and is dedicated to find an optimization of business performance. Finance has a deep dialogue with the business leaders about how to optimize their top line growth using analytic tools that support systematic data mining and Artificial Intelligence (AI).

Prescriptive Analytics goes beyond predicting future

outcomes to suggesting actions to benefit from the predictions and showing the implications of each decision option. Finance foresight impacts the future direction of the company on what changes to make so the business can achieve its target.

The Value of Next Generation Finance

The benefits of Next Generation Finance are exceedingly large in business performance and valuation, as well as, job security and satisfaction employee experience (with the latter two not to be understated). So, what's the cost of raising the analytics intelligence?

We'll discuss this in subsequent chapters, but the ROI on investments as assessed by all major consulting firms is at least 10:1. Further our research shows that companies that deliver consistent growth and earnings gain an increase of about 27% over the average forward PE multiple.

Finance is already spending considerably on information technology with marginal results. According to PWC studies[5] the median company IT spend in Finance is 0.55% of revenue, whereas top quartile companies spend 0.86%. However, these expenditures do not lift Finance much beyond Descriptive Analytics. Further, few Finance organizations get a seat-at-the-table as an enabler for decision making vs. merely having a monopoly on the financial data.

The corollary to spending on analytics is the cost for not spending on it. The notion of what you do not know can hurt you is indeed true. Companies waste time fixing items that they can't see are already mending, while not tending to close the barn door before the horse leaves on other areas. Predictive analytics can give views to the future that create unseen opportunities and mitigate unknown risks.

In a predictive example of heart-breaking agony, a major Las Vegas hotel/casino was given the prediction of the 2008 downturn some nine months earlier. The prediction was ignored, and no preparation was made to mitigate the impact. The moral of this story is predictions can be valuable – when acted upon!

Conclusion

Thus far, first generation Finance Transformation has focused on efficiencies and how to provide business leaders with faster, more accurate, and better information. Next Generation Finance enables Finance to provide insights and foresight on how and where to focus to drive top line growth.

Finance should no longer be satisfied to be seen as a provider of financial reporting, but an institution that delivers analytical insight and foresight that influence decision makers and impact the direction of the company. Next Generation Finance *(Figure 2-2)* and The Evolution of Analytics *(Figure 2-3)* and are both frameworks for how to advance Finance toward a culture of data driven decisions from analytics.

Both frameworks visualize how Finance moves from a trusted scorekeeper to a strategic partner. Next Generation Finance describes the journey through the additional capability needed for Finance to improve its skillset whereas the Evolution of Analytics describe which analytical techniques Finance needs to improve its toolbox.

3 ROADMAP TO AN ANALYTICS CULTURE

Without big data analytics, companies are blind and deaf –
Geoffrey Moore[1]

The Merriam Webster on-line dictionary defines "culture" as; the set of shared attitudes, values, goals, and practices that characterizes an institution or organization. Culture can be macro, as in a society, or micro, as in a business.

This book is about building a culture of "data driven decisions" within a business using analytics. It purports that Finance become the hub of analytics to partner with the business to deliver insights and foresight that impact decisions. The culture to be built has four key components of (1) Mindset, (2)

People, (3) Processes, and (4) Systems. These components, when aligned and implemented, institutionalize the practices and goals about data driven decisions for business optimization.

Much has been written about improving Finance business partnering and how Finance should move from the trusted scorekeeper in the back office to the front lines as the strategic partner. Finance wants and needs to have a seat-at-the-table for strategic and operational decisions, and to get there requires a disciplined, step by step journey that is benchmarked along the way to assure focus and prove attainment.

Gaining a seat at the table requires delivering *insights*; that is, to tell the business something that it both does not know and when known could influence or change a decision. Even more value is provided when *foresight* is delivered; that is, an often-reliable prediction of the future. As such, insights influence business decisions and foresight impacts business directions. The former provides knowledge about the past and the latter a forecast of the future (with all things being equal).

Creating a "culture" of data driven decisions with analytics requires a **Roadmap** to advance Finance to the world class strategic business partner. Depicted on Figure 3-1 below, are the four components of culture as a tightly integrated and interdependent framework.

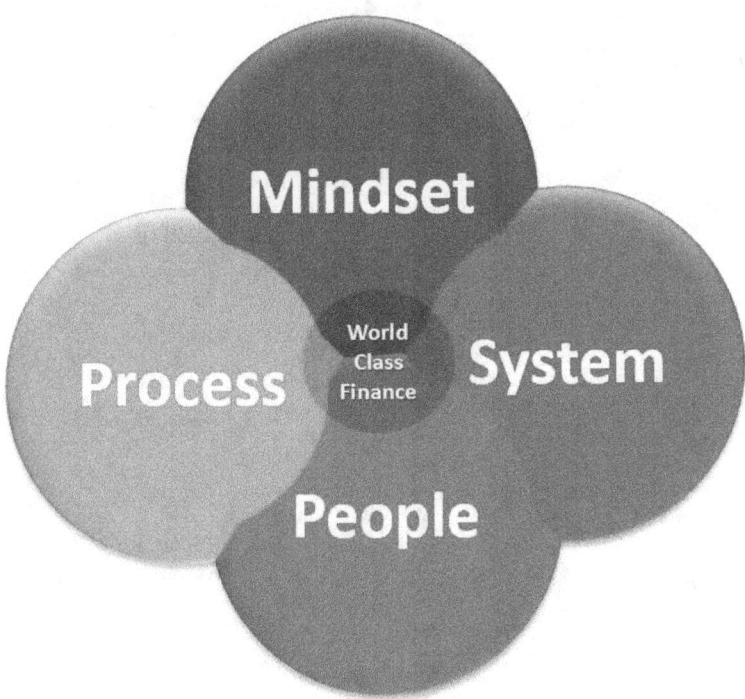

Figure 3-1: Analytics Culture Model

Mindset

Mindset regards Finance participation in the decision process. Each Mindset has a corresponding "Persona" and is related to a step on the stairs of Next Generation Finance (discussed in the previous chapter). We encapsulate four Mindsets with its Persona in Table 3-1 below:

Mindset	Persona	Deliverable
Support	Reporter	Accurate historical reporting
Contribute	Commentator	Accurate historical reporting delivered efficiently & with analysis
Influence	Advisor	Detail behavior of the trend & what's driving it
Impact	Strategist	Detail behavior of the trend & prediction of the future of the trend

Table 3-1: Mindset vs. Persona

The Persona of the **Reporter** has the Mindset to *Support* decisions by providing historical data requested by the business; e.g. sales are up 10% year to date over last year.

The **Commentator** has the Mindset to *Contribute* to decisions with some analysis of data; e.g. sales are up 10% but have been declining for the past three months caused by three stores in the chain. Here is where Finance makes its first leap out of the back-office Reporter.

The Commentator is focused to transition away from inefficient and often ineffective reporting, to <u>Eliminate</u> ineffective reports, <u>Elevate</u> regular reports to assure they yield information that contributes to better decisions, and <u>Automate</u> the production of regular reports to free bandwidth for data analysis.

The **Advisor** seeks to *Influence* decisions by giving insight not known; e.g. sales are up 10%, but have been down for the past three months, which decline has largely been driven by three large stores. The insight is that a competitor store has opened within three miles of our stores and the competitor's new store openings are negatively correlated to demand within a five-mile radius.

Finally, the **Strategist** Persona has the mindset to *Impact* decisions through predictive foresight; e.g. sales are up 10% this year but declining for the past three months, driven by three large stores, with the decline due to competitive store openings. However, unemployment is inversely correlated as a three-month leading indicator with demand in these three stores and, as unemployment has been dropping for the past three months, we predict sales will increase starting this month.

In short, the Reporter focus is on "What happened", the Commentator on "Where it happened", the Advisor on "Why did it happen" and the Strategist on "What might happen" and "How to make it happen".

People

People is about Finance, as a group, and how each individual views his role in participating in decisions. To go beyond a Reporter, there needs to be a "sufficient" number of people for analytics and an aligned Mindset to establish a culture of data driven decisions.

For example, in a large Finance group of a major healthcare provider, the CFO, while warm to the idea of analytics, never pressed for it. The same could be said for his direct reports, and the staff under them ran the gambit from "there's nothing we can get from analytics" to "that's interesting". The result was a group with unaligned Mindsets that could not advance beyond a Reporter Persona. As such, Finance did nothing more than to support decisions using spreadsheets with hindsight data.

It is important to note that Finance has more than one Persona. Finance is always the Reporter in delivering company financials, and there will be people who focus on this. However, if Finance wants a seat at the table it will need to go upstream in analytic intelligence and develop people with skills to become the Commentator, Advisor, and Strategist.

Processes

Processes regard the written procedures needed to institutionalize data driven decisions. Process are in two main groups of **Data Governance** and **Decision Governance.** The former is about assuring data used in decisions is accurate, complete, timely, and accessible; and note, Data Governance is *not* an IT function (which will be discussed in the chapter on Process). The latter regards the decision-making process itself to identify the decision-making participants, steps, and authorities.

Processes are often the weak link in the analytics culture chain, as processes are something that will be done later. However, "later" often doesn't arrive and when, in the normal course of business, people leave or change positions, their knowledge is lost, and analytics get derailed.

Systems

Systems is the hub of analytics and regards the technology employed by each Persona in the application of the Mindset, as listed on Table 3-2 below.

Mindset	Persona	Primary System
Support	Reporter	Excel & BI
Contribute	Commentator	Discovery & Visualization (DV)
Influence	Advisor	Desktop Statistical (DS) or Discovery, Visualization & Analytics (DVA)
Impact	Strategist	Discovery, Visualization & Analytics (DVA)

Table 3-2: Systems

As first described, spreadsheet and Business Intelligence (BI) tools are the bill-of-fare for the Reporter. These tools are aggregation to high-level and historically focused.

But these tools are largely inefficient to produce reports and many of these reports are ineffective. Reporting in these systems stagnates because it is difficult to maintain and modify. As such, many reports that have been created over time but, are no longer useful, remain in circulation. The Commentator requires efficient and effective reporting, and, for this, visualization tools are used. The

Advisor needs more insight from data and can use desktop statistical tools for high level and limited ad-hoc predictions, as well as, advanced analytics tools for larger volumes of data from multiple sources. The Strategist uses advanced analytics tools in a broader, deeper, and more sophisticated form, applying predictive analytics and Artificial Intelligence.

Conclusion

The coordinated combination of the four components of Mindset, People, Process, and System is crystallized on Figure 3-2 below. This is the *Roadmap* to build a *culture* of analytics of data driven decisions for Next Generation Finance.

Depending on the Analytics Intelligence that Finance wants to provide, measured on the left Y axis, it needs to align the four components in the analytics culture.

The X axis is the Mindset to add to decisions. As an example The Commentator is doing routine analysis that contribute decisions but has no analytics intelligence to influence or impact decisions.

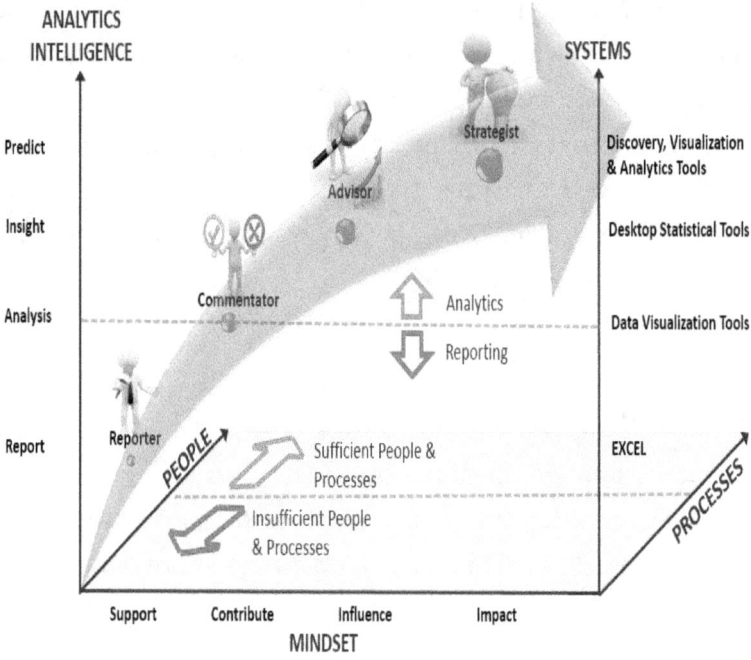

Figure 3-2: Roadmap to Analytics Culture

The right Y axis links the System to the Persona. Analytics starts from the Commentator, who do analysis using data visualization tools, and becomes more advanced as Finance progresses towards the Advisor and Strategist.

The two latter Personas provide Analytics intelligence in terms of insight and foresight to influence and enable business leaders to take better decisions to impact the execution and strategic direction of the company. With the Persona of a Strategist, the analytics intelligence becomes predictive and Finance needs access to advanced analytics tools of Discovery, Visualization & Analytics.

The two Z axis engage the People and Process, noting there needs to be a sufficient number of people and written processes to institutionalize, and sustain a data driven decision culture.

4 MINDSET

The Roadmap to a culture of analytics for data driven decisions starts with building and aligning the Mindset to decision making. The Mindset Model, depicted on Figure 4-1 below, operates with four Personas of a Finance organization; from **Reporter** to **Commentator** to **Advisor** to **Strategist**.

Average Finance organizations spend time on the left side of the Mindset Model while World Class Finance spend the majority of its time on the right side.

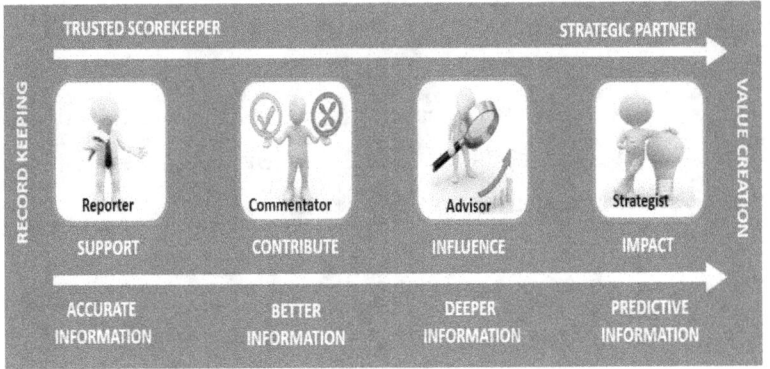

Figure 4-1: Mindset Model

To transition from the hindsight looking Reporter to the foresight looking predictive powerhouse Strategist, Finance needs to advance through the four roles moving from left to right. As discussed later, it is important to understand that Finance cannot be a Strategist without mastering the other three roles.

Note, Finance does not have to rise to the Strategist, as this Persona may not fit with the overall attitudes of the business. This does not connote failure. It is simply a recognition of what can be done as driven by the leadership of the company. However, all companies *should* be able to have Finance rise to the Advisor.

Reporter

The Reporter supports the business by providing reports containing hindsight information. The Reporter understands and utilizes financial reporting systems and establishes processes that ensure compliance. This Persona has demonstrated expertise with spreadsheets and spends much time capturing data from different BI data cubes/spreadsheets/transactional sources to consolidate into other spreadsheets.

Reporters are focused on delivering timely, accurate, and accessible financial information and communicate in a clean understandable fashion. The Reporter has limited business acumen and often operates as a back-office function with the primary goal to generate reports that are numbers "heavy" and with limited commentary.

Commentator

The Commentator adds visualization to reporting to explain trends and movements in performance. Data is turned into information (beyond high-level variance analysis) through detail explanation of the historical trends and deviations.

Finance, at this level, constantly updates its knowledge of the latest reporting tools and techniques and has automated and standardized reporting by using Centers of Excellence and Data Visualization tools. The Commentator performs analysis and identifies improvements in the business that drive better decisions that improve performance.

The Commentator secures alignment from the lines of business and seeks opportunities to collaborate and grow skills by involving others as necessary. Commentators form strong relationships with business leaders to build an understanding of the operations, as well as, to align communication to deliver a clear and transparent message.

The Commentator holds himself accountable for information shared and, contributes to decisions by describing deviations in the current performance to benchmarks and summarizing key points.

It is important to understand that most Finance organizations don't journey beyond the Commentator Mindset, which means Finance has limited capabilities of challenging and influencing strategic decisions.

Advisor

The Advisor identifies issues and opportunities by using more complete knowledge of internal data, competitors, and the market to provide insight to business leaders that influence their decision making. The Advisor expands his focus to bring insight to top line performance.

Insight is information that the business does not know; e.g. correlating between the current performance and other financial or non-financial data. The Advisor use multi-source data and analytics to explain why things have happened.

The Advisor develops a range of analysis/options/paths to achieve business objectives within a changing environment. For example, Advisors perform scenario analysis using internal and external market data to quantify sensitivities. Finance, at this level, use desktop statistical or big data analytics tools to generate statistical analytics in an effort to tell the business something it does not know.

Advisors collaborate with both business and other Finance teams to learn about leading analytical tools and techniques and obtain business knowledge to drive more complex analytics that create the insights that support business needs.

Strategist

The Strategist impact business decisions by generating the most advanced forms of analytics; e.g. predictive and prescriptive analytics to explain what is likely to happen and how to make it happen.

He provides advanced analytics from simple smoothing to the most sophisticated techniques like data mining using machine learning, Systematic Intelligence™, and other Artificial Intelligence (AI).

The Strategist is seen as a key and influential member of the business leadership team who provide analytical insight and foresight that impact strategic direction.

Strategists use Discovery, Visualization & Analytic tools with AI to understand competitors, customers, and vendors' strength and weaknesses and use that insight to predict future events and performance. When modeling, the Strategist can simulate high/low cases from Monte Carlo simulations.

The Strategist is a visionary that inspires and engages people. He is seen as a role model and thought leader, both internal and external, as he innovates Finance and encourages entrepreneurship.

The Strategist is often seen as the glue in who holds self and others accountable for delivering shareholder value and understands how strategic decisions affect the future for the business.

Capability Model

The journey of moving from the Reporter towards the Strategist starts with an understanding of the capabilities needed to advance through the four Personas.

The capabilities of Basics, Acumen, Intelligence, and Strategy defines the elements to achieve Next Generation

Finance as described in Chapter 2. Linking these capabilities with the Personas in the Mindset Model, gives Finance a framework of where to focus to advance towards the Strategic Partner.

In the Capability Model in Figure 4-2 below, it is important to understand that all Personas need **Basics.** As Finance advances its Mindset towards the Strategic Partner, it adds the capabilities of Acumen, Intelligence, and Strategy.

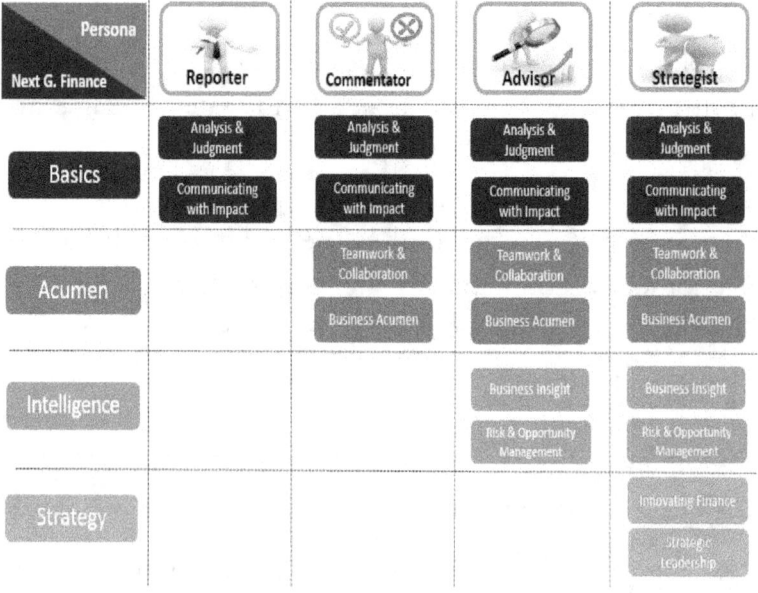

Persona / Next G. Finance	Reporter	Commentator	Advisor	Strategist
Basics	Analysis & Judgment	Analysis & Judgment	Analysis & Judgment	Analysis & Judgment
	Communicating with Impact	Communicating with Impact	Communicating with Impact	Communicating with Impact
Acumen		Teamwork & Collaboration	Teamwork & Collaboration	Teamwork & Collaboration
		Business Acumen	Business Acumen	Business Acumen
Intelligence			Business Insight	Business Insight
			Risk & Opportunity Management	Risk & Opportunity Management
Strategy				Innovating Finance
				Strategic Leadership

Figure 4-2: Capability Model

Business Acumen includes a deep understanding of the business operation, to an advanced level of understanding the competitive landscape, and using that knowledge to provide analytical insight.

Most Finance organizations do not advance beyond the Commentator and thereby don't add Intelligence and Strategy to its capabilities.

However, for Finance groups that do advance, **Intelligence** includes insight like providing correlations between financial data and non-financial data sources along with risk and opportunity management including an understanding of how to use Monte Carlo Simulation to provide probabilities of reaching high or low case forecasts.

Strategy includes innovating Finance and strategic leadership, and involves Finance being seen as a thought leader, both internally as well as externally, and strategic decisions are not being taken without Finance involvement.

An example of some of the capabilities to be measured for each Persona is visualized in Appendix A. The Capability Model is also a way to assess exactly at which level a Finance organization operates, as well as, which capabilities to improve to more towards the Strategist.

From Average to World Class Finance

Below, on Table 4-1, we reference Next Generation

Finance and the Evolution of Analytics (both described in Chapter 2) with the progression through Mindset and corresponding Systems.

Area	From Average to World Class
Evolution of Analytics	Explaining what and where it happened to why, what might, and how can we make it happen
Next Generation Finance	Improve from basic financial capabilities to adding Acumen, Intelligence and Strategy
Mindset	Moving from Support to Contribute to Influence to Impact decisions
Systems	Improve toolbox from Excel to Data Visualization to Desktop Statistical to Discovery, Visualization and Analytics Tools

Table 4-1: From Average to World Class

The Finance maturity is measured against Figure 4-3. Finance moves from average to world class by improving its Capabilities, Mindset, and System tools.

A description of how to advance the Mindset is depicted in Figure 4.1, Mindset Model. The advancement of Capabilities in Figure 4.2, Capability Model. Systems will be described in detail in Chapter 7.

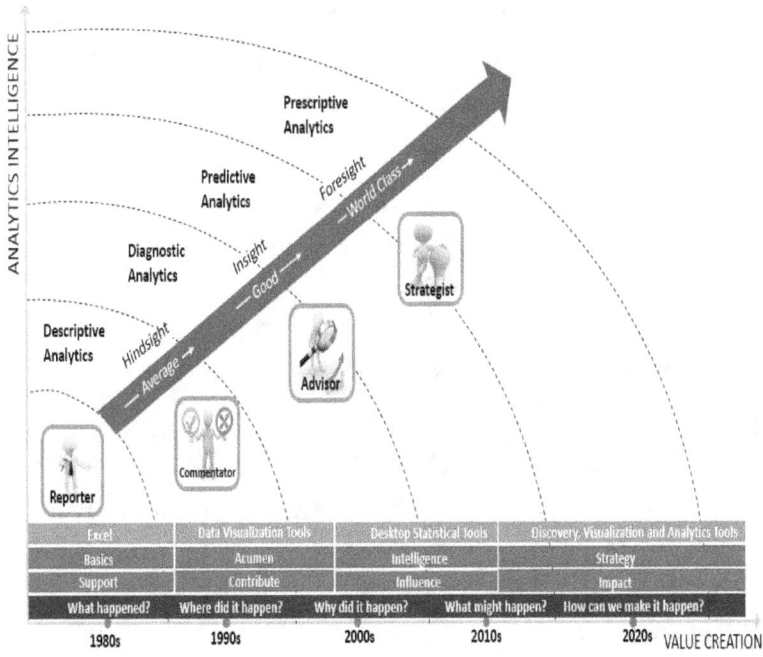

Figure 4-3: From Average to World Class

To summarize Personas, the **Reporter** possess basic capabilities and supports the business by providing reports containing hindsight information. The Reporter utilizes financial systems and establishes processes that ensure compliance. Reporters have expertise with spreadsheets and spend most time capturing data from different BI data cubes/spreadsheets/transactional sources to consolidate into other spreadsheets.

The **Commentator** has enhanced capabilities to include business acumen. The Commentator adds visualization to reporting to explain trends and movements in the performance. The Commentator contributes by turning data into information beyond high-level variance analysis through detail explanation of the historical trends and deviations.

The **Advisor** identifies issues and opportunities by using expanded internal data and market intelligence to provide insight to business that influence their decision making. The Advisor expands his focus to top line performance.

The **Strategist** impacts strategic direction, as the Strategist is capable of generating the most advanced forms of analytics; e.g. predictive and prescriptive analytics to explain what is likely to happen and how to make it happen.

Beside from having strategic leadership, the Strategist also innovates by utilizing the most advanced tools of Discovery, Visualization and Analytics along with Artificial Intelligence (AI). The latter technology can elevate Finance, enabling both deeper predictive analytics and developing heretofore multiple scenarios for risk mitigation planning and opportunity optimization.

Research

Our research, on Figure 4-4 below, shows that most Finance organizations spend some two-thirds of its time gathering data, reporting a analyzing on historical performance. This leaves precious little time to high value analytics. To free time to do analytics, Finance can utilize data visualization tools to reduce the time to prepare standard reports.

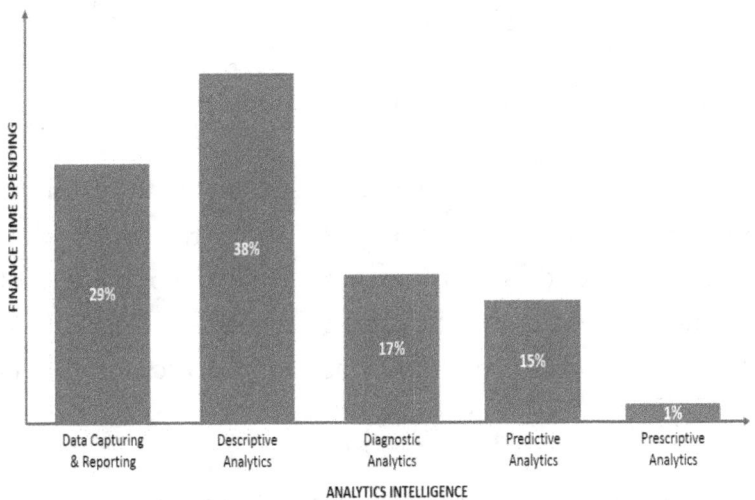

Figure 4-4: Expenditure of Time

Further our survey shows, in Figure 4-5 below, that less than 1% of Finance organizations see itself as Strategists. Some 33% self-classify as Advisors, while 50% are Commentators. The remaining 17% consider themselves Reporters delivering timely and accurate standard hindsight reporting.

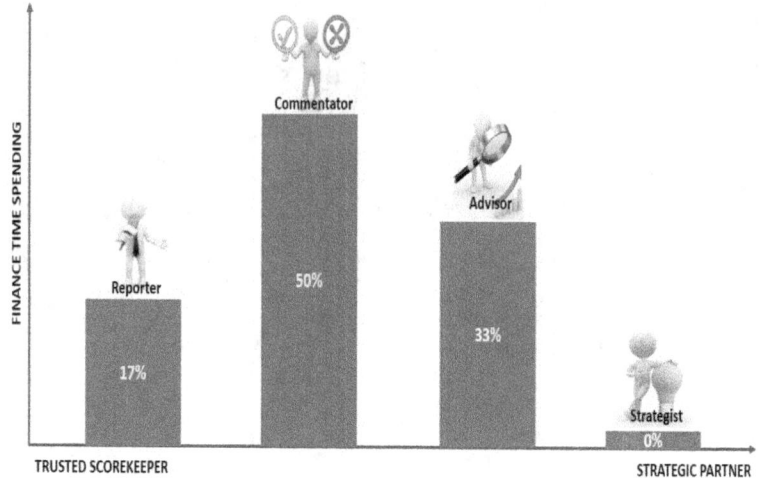

Figure 4-5: Finance Personas

Note, no Finance organization can act as Advisor or Strategist without mastering the Reporter and Commentator roles. Business leaders will be open to trust Finance advanced analytics and predictions, if and only if, Finance has delivered reporting on historical numbers timely, accurately, and accessibly.

There is quite a way to go for most Finance groups to become the world class Strategic Partners, but Finance has the interest and intent to move beyond the trusted scorekeeper. Our research shows that 67% aim to become Strategists, 22% Advisors, 17% Commentator but, most important, no one wants to remain Reporters. This is a good direction!

Conclusion

Aligning Next Generation Finance and Evolution of Analytics to the Mindset framework describes how Finance moves from average to world class. Finance always has the base function as a **Reporter.** As Finance advances it moves into the role of the **Commentator** by automating reporting to free time for analysis. The Commentator contributes to decisions by turning data into information and communicating in the language of the business.

The **Advisor** provides advanced analytics to generate deeper information and insight that influence decision makers. To reach world class, Finance evolves to the **Strategist** to challenge the business through innovative thinking and use of advanced analytic tools to predictive events, risks, and opportunities.

Having the right Mindset and access to leading tools and techniques enables Finance to deliver deeper and predictive information to transform from a spreadsheet-driven accounting center to a value-add predictive analytics hub.

5 PEOPLE

Coming together is a beginning. Keeping together is progress. Working together is success – Henry Ford[1]

In building the culture of analytic decision making, the component of People considers their qualification to fulfill the Mindset, the alignment of People with the aspirational Mindset, and the number of People to sufficiently achieve the Mindset. Therefore, this chapter constructs the People, characteristics, and headcount needed for each Mindset Persona and the overall Mindset goal of Finance.

Figure 5-1 below, asks at each level, the Mindset to decision making to assess the alignment. Specifically, a manager may have a desire to be an Advisor, but this will require analytic tools. If his Director has no affinity to anything more than a Mindset of Reporter, then no budget for analytic tools will be allocated, thus leaving the manager incapable of being an Advisor. In time, the manager will become frustrated and leave the company.

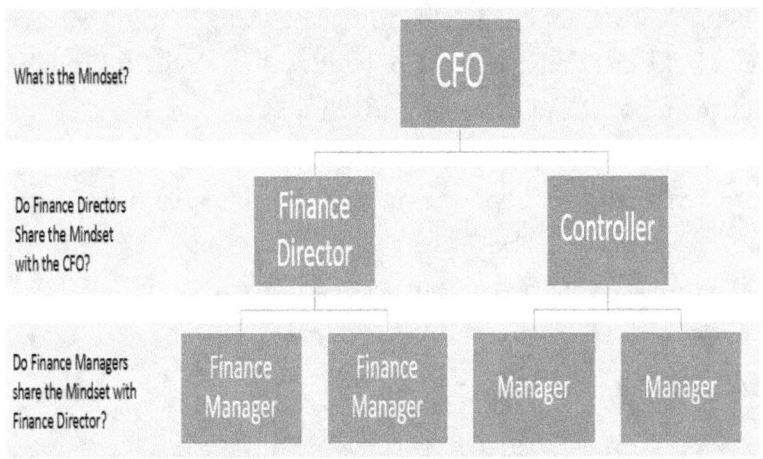

Figure 5-1: Mindset Alignment

However, Finance can and does have more than one Persona. For routine financial reports, Finance is a Reporter. If Finance wants a "seat at the table", it will need to advance to the Advisor. As such, the more advanced Finance wants to be in delivering insights, the greater the breadth of Personas Finance will need to deploy.

A Reporter need only Excel to produce reports and the discipline to assure reports are accurate and delivered in time for those who use them. The Reporter is not concerned if the production of reports is efficient or even if the reports are effective for operations in making their decisions.

However, an Advisor requires an analytic tool and a capacity to analyze and distill data into a meaningful summary that can be consumed for data driven decisions. As such, if Finance, as a group, aspires to be the Advisor it would need at least two headcounts, one to deliver reporting and the other for advising.

But why can an Advisor not be a Reporter, or a Reporter be an Advisor? Because the skill sets are significantly different. Table 5-1 below relates Personas with skills.

Skills	Reporter	Commentator	Advisor	Strategist
Excel Expert	X	X		
Auditor Skill	X	X		
Business Collaborator		X	X	X
Data Analyst Skill			X	X
Story Teller Skill			X	X
Develop Insight			X	X
Develop Foresight				X

Table 5-1: Persona Skills

A Reporter needs to be an expert in Excel with the characteristic of an auditor to assure reporting is accurate and complete. The Commentator has the profile of a

Reporter with the added skill of a modicum of capability as a data analyst and a rudimentary ability to collaborate with the business to learn its needs in order to deliver reporting for effective decision making.

The Advisor and Strategist only need Excel proficiency but must be deeply skilled in data analysis. Further, Advisors talk to the business with the knowledge of the business. They have the ability to deliver insights and tell the "story" through visualization and analytics that the business can consume to make decisions that optimize performance.

As such, the Advisor teaches the business about its past performance, whereas the Strategist predicts what the business faces if its future operations are not altered. Accordingly, the task at hand is to understand how to develop and align people in Finance about the individual and group goals.

The Reporter

The Reporter delivers accurate, complete, and timely regular reporting. The Reporter does not have to be efficient and, typically, is not because he most often uses spreadsheets largely or exclusively for planning and reporting. The Reporter also provides operations with ad-hoc reporting on historical data that is driven by questions generated from the regular operational reports.

Responses to ad-hoc reporting are also largely done via spreadsheets.

Responsibilities: Deliver regular and ad-hoc financial and operational reports that are accurate, complete, timely, and accessible as the trusted score-keeper. Oddly, the Reporter does not concern himself with delivering reports efficiently or that are effective for decision-making.

Reports are of historical performance. Forecasts and budgets are manually prepared from guesses and lack objectivity of statistical analysis. Reporters deliver the key financial data for the business that no company can function without.

Characteristics: An excellent eye for detail with the discipline of an auditor. All items on reports must tick-and-tie so consumers of the reports remain confident of the information thereon. Reporters tend to be introverted and prefer not to interface with operations and instead focus to deliver that which has been specified.

Skills/Experience: An Excel expert usually with proficiency in Access. Adept at pulling data from transactional systems, data warehouse, and BI data marts that are then combined in spreadsheets. A degree in finance or accounting and experience working in an accountancy firm.

Headcount: Since efficiency of preparing reports is not a requirement, the number of people can be relatively large. Headcount depends on scope of work, efficiency of reporting, and industry. For example, an $800 million healthcare provider used an FP&A staff of some 25 people, whereas a $400 million division of a Fortune 500 technology company's staff was about 35.

Benchmarks: Here it is about accuracy of data, timeliness of delivery, and access by those who need it; i.e. getting accurate data at the right time to the right people.

The Commentator

The Commentator efficiently delivers regular and ad-hoc reports through automation, eliminates unnecessary reports, and assures reports are elevated to be effective for operation's use. As mentioned in Chapter 4, Mindset, Commentators seek to Automate, Eliminate, and Elevate reporting. Commentators are fewer in headcount than Reporters. In fact, in the 21st Century, there is little reason that all regular reports are not largely, or completely automated, and ad-hoc reports are largely self-service.

Responsibilities: Same as the Reporter but delivers regular reporting through automation of data pulls and report generation. Reports that cannot be done via BI, visualization, or analytic tools are to be changed to accommodate automation. The notion that a report format cannot be changed is simply not so. Consumers of reporting are not stupid, but they can be lazy. As such, Commentators must push consumers into rational reporting and in turn give them better reports.

To deliver reports that are more effective for decision-making, the Commentator builds relationships in the organization by being able to talk the business language and understand the business model to better support and contribute to decision making. He delivers value-add with better information than just standard variance analysis and cost center controls.

The Commentator should have regular quarterly meetings with operations to assure the efficacy of reports and discard reports that have no value. The key question to ask operations is; what decisions do you make from current reports? Identify any reports that should be added or changed and specify how reporting is effectively providing information to optimize the business.

Characteristics: Same as the Reporter but is out going with a thirst for efficiency and the desire to understand the business and how to drive better business decisions. The Commentator also wants to drive ad-hoc reporting to the consumer level through self-service tools.

Skills/Experience: Same as Reporter but who has used visualization tools for delivering reports.

Headcount: The number of Commentators should be less than half the number of Reporters.

Benchmarks: Commentators will spend no more than 50% of their time on regular and ad-hoc reports and will enable operations with self-service tools that answer 80% of operation's queries. Spreadsheets will still be a primary tool, but not the only tool, and spreadsheet use will drop by at least 50%.

The Advisor & Strategist

The Advisor and Strategist are higher cost people, fewer in number, and deliver high value through sophisticated analytics. Every major report from every major consulting firm has quantified the ROI on investments from analytics systems and practices as at least 10:1.

From our experience, this is a floor return for analytics. These Personas take Finance to world class by providing a depth of insight heretofore unknown to the business.

The Advisor and Strategist main difference is the Advisor provides insights of the past whereas the Strategist offers foresight to the future.

Responsibilities: The Advisor and Strategist builds relationships in the organization and understands the business operation to *influence and impact*, respectively, decision making by identifying issues and opportunities. Advisor and Strategist have access to multi-sources of data and use various statistics and diagnostic analytics to generate *insight and foresight* that is used for data driven decisions.

By building relationships in the organization and being able to talk the business language and understand the business model, these Personas can better influence and impact decision making.

Characteristics: These Personas think broader than just "what" is happening and "where", to understand "why" it is happening. For example, sales can be down as a customer is buying less but why is the customer buying less? Is it due to customer satisfaction, new salesman with less experience than prior salesmen, conditions in the market where the customer operations could be down, or overall market conditions, GDP, unemployment, etc.?

For the Strategist, broader thinking than just "why" it is happening to understand "what might" happen in the future.

For example, validate if the sales forecast is realistic by using multiple forecast techniques like smoothing, leading Indicators, conversion rates, etc. Challenge and influence which deals are at risk of not closing; i.e. those deals in the sales forecast that don't follow a "profile" with high propensity of closing. Simulate ranges of outcome with Monte Carlo analysis to calculate high and low cases, and probability curves to give all a fair challenge.

Both personas have the characteristic of a consultant to listen, advise, and help engineer better outcomes and optimize operations.

Skills/Experience: A capability to do statistical analysis, and an analytic thought process combined with a personality to interact with the business and reduce the complex to that which can be understood by the non-analyst.

This is a position well suited for the college graduate in engineering, or economics, or digital marketing with the combination of being outgoing, as well as, mathematical. Here, experience with a consulting firm is a plus.

Headcount: To build a culture of data driven decisions from analytics will take the minimum of two from Finance and five business consumers. Anything less cannot sustain a culture of analytics and is subject to evaporation from attrition.

Benchmarks: 10:1 ROI is a base.

Alignment – The Key to Finance Group Success

Persona misalignment is the largest cause of failure to implement a culture of data driven decisions through analytics. If the CFO thinks one way and the staff another, job dissatisfaction will result, and turn-over will follow.

As such, each level of Finance should be clear to its Persona and aligned to deliver to it. Finance can and does have more than one Persona and, therefore, assure the People in each Persona share the same characteristics and skills. Remember too, it is not the level of the Finance professional that define the persona it is the mindset. As such a Vice President can be a Reporter and a Analyst can be a Strategist.

One way to assure People alignment is to align Persona and training. Table 5-2 below to depict baseline training programs.

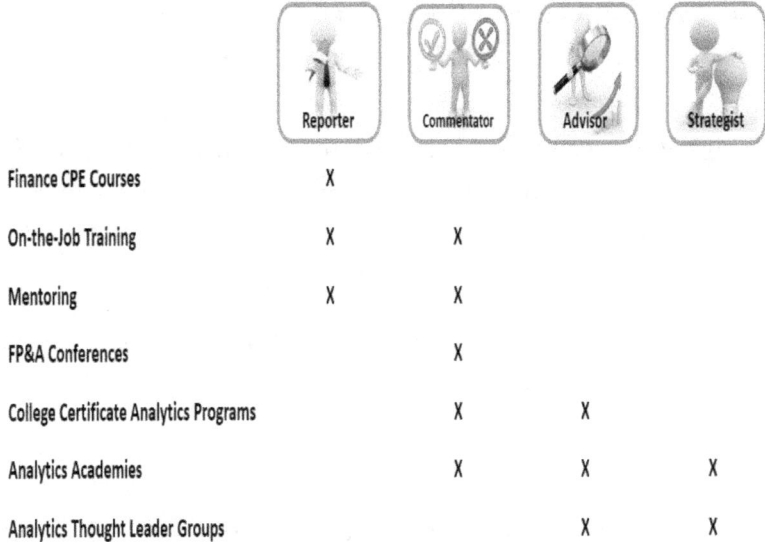

	Reporter	Commentator	Advisor	Strategist
Finance CPE Courses	X			
On-the-Job Training	X	X		
Mentoring	X	X		
FP&A Conferences		X		
College Certificate Analytics Programs		X	X	
Analytics Academies		X	X	X
Analytics Thought Leader Groups			X	X

Table 5-2: Persona Training

Environment for Successful People

A culture of decisions through analytics will expose Finance but may flaws in People and Processes. This will be uncomfortable at the beginning and a cause of resistance to analytics. As such, there are a few key "people" practices to employ when implementing analytics.

It has been said, "praise in public, punish in private". This is a good mantra to assure people feel respected, are not embarrassed, and have room for error. Even more important, an environment must encourage innovation and be welcoming to criticism that helps advance the individual and group. Below are the key points for people practice on the road to analytics:

- Promote Candor – to deliver unvarnished thinking and mitigate people having to "read between the lines" to discern thoughts.

- Kill Political Correctness – as PC is the biggest killer of innovation. When every word uttered is spoken in fear of offending someone then the status quo is maintained, and progress is muted.

- Open Data Access – as the more who see and use data the better the data becomes. Too often folks that "control" data use it as a point of power or to hide from errors. The former creates false job security, and the latter is the excuse that the data was wrong to deflect from blame.

- Mistakes Are Good – we're all human and mistakes are inevitable be they errors or omissions. Therefore, embrace these as the opportunity to fix and be better.

- Embrace "Bad" Results – as these are opportunities for improvement. Hiding the "misses" only prolongs the behavior that created them.

The Trap

Too many reports generated by Finance have limited effectiveness. For example, repeated requests were made of a Finance group of a major healthcare system to meet with Operations to discuss reporting. Finance believed the reports it provided were what Operations wanted. After *years* of insistence, Finance and Operations met to review reports.

The dialogue between the groups was shocking and long overdue. Operations was asked to confirm that Finance reports were what they wanted. However, Operations said they did not use much of the reports because they had limited value. When asked why they received the reports in the current form, they responded because Finance gave it to them that way!

This is typical of a great many companies. Finance thinks its reports are what Operations wants and Operations thinks it was Finance who decided the reports they get. So, who is right? Both are.

Most reports began years ago and simply do not change, as they are largely in big and complicated spreadsheets and BI tools, they can be hard to change . . . so the reports don't. Finance wastes its valuable time in preparing reports that Operations gains marginal value from. Therefore, for Finance to go from average to world class this reporting trap must be avoided.

Don't Waste High IQ People on Low IQ Tasks

As mentioned in Chapter 4, Mindset, Finance typically

spends two-thirds of its time data loading and compiling regular reports. This is taking high IQ talent to low IQ copy/paste spreadsheet compilation vs. spending high IQ time on high value data analytics.

The return on efficient and effective reporting is large and measurable. For example, at a Forecasting & Analytics Summit[2], a Director of FP&A at a major consumer credit company, explained her group cut regular reports from 1,300 to 600 and eliminated 400 hours in report production effort.

How was this accomplished? Simply by Finance becoming a Commentator and asking the operational groups for those reports not being used or of little use. Freeing 400 hours from "mindless" spreadsheet compilation enabled attention to higher value functions, and the first step that followed, was to gain knowledge into the application of analytics for Finance.

Analytics for Career Advancement & Job Satisfaction

It is astonishing to think that Excel is so widely used in Finance, for so long, and for so many manners of reporting and analysis. While Excel is a wondrous tool, it is not equipped to do most of the enterprise class applications it is doing today (for a wide variety of well-known reasons we need not delve into here). However, Excel's ubiquitous days may be nearing its peak.

Millennials are now filling the ranks of companies and are only using Excel because of the Excel culture of the prior generation, not because they have an affinity to this tool. For example, one Millennial at a major transportation company, noted that if it were up to him, he would be using Python, as that is what he learned in college.

Millennials read, shop, and socialize on-line. Excel does not fit with the millennial lifestyle. As such, change is in the wind. It will be driven by Millennials as they take charge. Their technology preference will be adopted, and just as important, their need to abandon copy/past routine of spreadsheet reporting and into more interesting data analytics.

Beyond Millennials, all people in Finance need to think broader than just "what" is happening, and advance to understand "why" it is happening. If Sales are down it is more than customers are buying less. We need to know *why* the customer is buying less. We need to find the analytical correlations of customer satisfaction, salesman experience, conditions in the market, and external drivers (like unemployment) to explain the sales drop.

Finance people need also to ponder the future; that is, "what might" happen. Using analytics, we can make forecasts and determine if those forecasts are reasonable, identify the sales deals that follow the pattern to close vs. a salesman "feeling" it will close, find customers with a propensity to churn to take proactive steps to retain, and many other examples.

All of this is exciting and high value. It is what high IQ folk want to do. It will be how they advance their careers as they become part of determining the strategic direction of their companies.

Conclusion

One man does not make an analytics culture, it takes people. As a group, the CFO is responsible for determining the level of analytics intelligence his group aspires to. And, he must drive his group to that Persona. Just "wanting" to be a Strategist is insufficient.

6 PROCESSES

[It's] difficult for [firms] to capitalize on disruptive innovations
[as] their processes . . . that make them good at the existing
business actually make them bad at competing for the disruption –
Clayton Christensen[1]

Christensen observed that good companies build efficient processes that lock them into technologies they cannot innovate out of. In implementing analytics, processes are essential to building a culture of analytics. As we refer herein, Processes are the **written** procedures that **institutionalize** the culture for data driven decisions. Without written procedures an analytics culture cannot be sustained and will suffer from the attrition of people that naturally occurs.

The two areas of process are **Data Governance** and **Decision Governance**. The former assures data is accurate, complete, timely, and accessible. The latter assures the inputs and authorities for data driven decisions. Appendix B provides a sample framework for Data and Decision Governance.

The cornerstones of good governance are that (1) management make personnel time available and with incentive to attend to the actions of governance, (2) management uses the analytics subject to governance, (3) there are defined roles and responsibilities of governance memorialized in written procedure, and (4) periodic measurements are made to assure the goals of governance and continuous business improvement through analytical decisions.

Data Governance

The working definition of Data Governance is:

The management process of data to assure it is timely, complete, accurate, and accessible for reporting and analytics to its intended business purpose.

Data Governance is not a full-time job in Finance or Operations but a part of each person's job and can be divided into:

1. People who "own" data
2. People who "analyze" data
3. People who "consume" analytics of data

Owners are responsible for data accuracy and timeliness. **Analyzers** are responsible for data completeness and accessibility. **Consumers** are responsible to make decisions utilizing the data analysis. These responsibilities compromise a coordinated approach to Data Governance. Table 6-1 below lists the goals, deliverables, and benchmarks for the sufficiency of the data.

Data Goals	Data Deliverable	Data Benchmark
Data Timeliness	Right Time Availability	Sufficient Reaction Time (in case of problems pulling & preparing the data)
Complete & Accurate	Right Data, No Errors	Free from Errors & Missing Data
Data Accessibility	Data for All Who Need	Ease of Access & Use

Table 6-1: Data Goals

Important to note, is that Data Governance is **not** an IT responsibility. IT handles data security but IT has nary a clue as what data is relevant, accurate, or complete for making business decisions.

Its role in Data Governance is assuring IT is highly

responsive and does not create bureaucracy that delays requests for changes in data or systems that support Data Governance. Below are three rules for IT:

- People – no armies, no more than one interface per database
- Processes – no bureaucracy, no more than one request form per database
- Promptness – no delay, turn-around time must be measured in hours or days

The foundation of Data Governance is written processes to assure institutionalization. This is not hard, but nearly all organizations are excessively lax in this regard.

As such, the normal occurrence of attrition and reorganization becomes acid that erodes the efficiency and effectiveness of the culture of data driven decisions because institutional knowledge is lost when the people who possess it are gone. Written processes should follow a flow and framework as reflected on the Table in Table 6-2 below.

Process Flow	Framework
High Level Data Process Overview	Identifies the sources of data, owners of data, times of data update, times of data pull, activities for data preparation to make it load ready for the reporting and analytic tools, tests for data accuracy, and authorities for correcting data or expanding the data pull
Sub Process Detail	Any of the processes in the Overview that require detail explanation or elaboration
Production Schedule Overview	Delineates the times of data pull and loading into the reporting and analytic systems
Production Update & Details	Delineates the update of reporting and analytical systems and feedback for data correction or data expansion

Table 6-2: Data Governance Procedure Framework

Data Governance can have a rocky roll-out, so there are a few rules to highlight. First, it is *very important* that data errors be positively embraced, and data sources be open. Too often people shelter the data they are responsible for as a means to protect their position or to blame the data when targets are missed. This is excessively bad, as people are not held accountable and needed data is not improved.

Second, and as serious, is when people are punished for data errors. Punishment should follow when errors are routine due to continuing (not one time) carelessness – not for honest mistakes. Until the Creator makes humans perfect, mistakes will be part of the landscape. Therefore, finding bad data as soon as possible should be a point of pride. Better data yields better analytics and better decisions.

Data Governance Best Practices

Garbage in garbage out is what we hear regarding data quality that it often paralyzes analytic implementations. IT is called to "clean" the data before the commencement of data driven decisions. Consultants are engaged and armies of people, flow charts, reports, and years of effort follow. All a burdensome and inefficient exercise with low efficacy that wastes inordinate amounts of time and capital.

Bad data is found from using the data by the people who know the data and those are the users of it! Therefore, proceed with your analytics and let the People, Process, and Systems uncover and fix that data that needs fixing. You'll find that the overwhelming vast majority of your data is right. This is the fastest and most effective form of data cleansing and developing good Data Governance.

Decision Governance

The working definition of Decision Governance is:

Management process of decisions to assure it's driven by analytics to make better decisions that improve business performance.

Process Flow	Framework
High Level Decision Overview	Identifies the analytics input, receivers of the analytics, times analytics are delivered, how the analytics are used in decisions, authorities for making decisions, and process to identify data errors, questions about the data, and need for additional data or analytics
Sub Process Detail	Any of the processes in the Overview that require detail explanation or elaboration
Production Schedule Overview	Delineates the times of analytics needs to be delivered and the form and medium
Production Update & Details	Delineates the update of reporting and analytical systems and feedback for data correction or data expansion

Table 6-3: Data Governance Procedure Framework

Most small decisions are reactive, and large decisions emotional. Neither leads to business optimization. Decision Governance are written processes (similar to Table 6-2) that articulate how data analysis in incorporated in decision making. Table 6-3 above presents the framework for Decision Governance.

Just having an analytic tool with a man who sits about waiting to be asked a question, is neither a culture of analytic decisions nor of much value, as it is not part of a formalized decision process. As such

Decision Governance involves:
- Identify the analytics used to make decisions
- Timing for delivery of analytics and to who
- The process of using analytics
- The decision authorities

The data used to make decisions constantly evolves, as the more that is learned from data analysis, the more it inspires questions that drive more analysis and, hence, data. As such, regular meetings should occur to assess data sufficiency to both discontinue unnecessary data and identify new data needs. These results should feed-back into Data Governance.

Timing of when data is needed and who are the recipients feeds the Data Governance process as well. Analytical decision making can be analogous to a Just-In-Time supply chain; i.e. to have the most current data analysis, delivered to the right people, at the right time.

The process of using analytics for decisions and decisions authorities relate, in the former, to the inputs for the decision process and, in the latter, to who makes the decisions.

For example, a manufacturing company is considering adding a new production line. To do such, the company requires its demand forecast to show a sustained level of growth.

The company begins with an AI generated forecast to assure the objectivity in an 18-month rolling forecast. Further, the company defines sustained growth when the rolling 18-month forecast shows at least 2% growth for 6 consecutive forecasts.

If the objective statistical forecast meets this threshold then Operations is notified to trigger a recommended investment in another production line. The decision process follows that the Operations team verifies the forecast analysis then passes a recommended investment decision to the VP of Operations that will be reviewed in the quarterly capex planning meeting.

Note, in this example, verification involves finding a 9-month leading external indicator (e.g. GDP) that is used to assess the reasonableness of the forecast. The purpose of verification is to utilize further objective quantitative statistical analysis to compliment the AI forecasting.

Also note, human knowledge of the future is part of the process. Forecasts can be adjusted by humans who have definitive knowledge of the future that is not known by past data. Further, when conflicts arise between human and machine this is to be embraced. These differences create a dialogue of challenging outcomes, knowledge, and assumptions. This *will* produce better results when done *honestly*.

Decision Governance Best Practice

It is *very important* that predictive analytics is incorporated into decisions and understood that a high value of predictions is to give contrast to human intuition. This contrast should be positively embraced to critically talk through areas where analytics doesn't agree with feelings.

Key to note is that all forecasts are wrong, it's just a matter of degree. As such, plan to the range of probable outcomes rather than a specific forecast. This will circumvent spending weeks following each quarter's end explaining why the actuals results did not exactly match the forecast. So long as outcomes fall within the probable planning range there is no need to expend time in variance analysis.

Analytical decisions are analogous to a Just-In-Time

supply chain; that is, to have the most current data analysis, delivered to the right people, at the right time. Decision Governance relates to both the analytics inputs for decisions and who makes decisions.

Failure is an Option – But Why?

Too many times, projects fail because there simply were no procedures. People were aligned and ready, precious capital spent on analytic systems, but no processes to institutionalize the Data and Decision Governance.

For example, in one retail company an analytical tool was bought, and a project well implemented. It thoughtfully established a baseline of the current monthly forecasting and decision process that use spreadsheets. Then, it specified the improvements that would be made to the process from using analytics to reduce the time and increase forecast accuracy. The software was configured and installed, people trained but, despite insistence to immediately create written processes, none were made.

A pilot test of the software was completed to assure the quality of the analytics but, a few weeks before the launch into operations, the analytics point-man was promoted. The next man to come in had no written processes to follow, and in short-suit the project was abandoned. A most avoidable outcome and a senseless waste of people and capital.

Failure was an option. The company continued doing rolling forecasts in spreadsheets – and achieving the same results – high level of effort to get spotty forecast accuracy.

Money was thrown away, but life went on. The Vice President who made the promotion and the analytics point-man are to blame . . . yes, blame. They pinched pennies to avoid spending on written processes, only to lose pounds and opportunity for material performance improvement.

Process Doesn't Punish Productivity - Executives Do

People often claim in frustration they have no time for the overhead of process; this will just add more work to an already compressed day. However, in an analytics culture, process brings discipline and organization that creates productivity. The productivity punishers are the executives!

Executives are inquisitive and have a thirst for information – this is good. However, they largely have no clue of the impact on productivity their queries have on their organization. So too, staff spends too much time making executive reports "pretty".

For example, in a Fortune 500 company an executive wanted a particular analysis of a capital project. All FP&A

stopped their regular work to focus on delivering reports the next week. Staff worked over the weekend, which included the wasted tasks of putting logos, colors, and other images on spreadsheets and PowerPoint reports – all of which added NO value to the content of the information.

A great job by all, all for a 60-minute meeting!

Subsequently, FP&A fell behind its regular work, which required another weekend to catch-up. To add insult to injury, the information could have been done with self-service tools . . . if only the executives would use them.

It is OK to demand more from people, but only when needed. Taxing people's time too often becomes disrespectful and can be demoralizing.

The solution is four-fold (1) executives must be conscious of the impact of their requests for information, (2) executives must become tech savvy and use tools that can be responsive to 80% of their queries, (3) executives must direct that time is not wasted on making reports "pretty" and to focus on function not aesthetics, and (4) Finance and Operations need push back on executive requests to protect the productivity of their staff and assure the requests are such that cannot otherwise be attained.

Conclusion

Data and Decision Governance processes are essential to the culture of data driven decisions through analytics but is often the area companies ignore in implementing analytics. It is not that companies cannot develop these written processes but, too often, chose not to. Either for the time that it takes someone(s) to build processes with internal resources, and/or the budget to spend on external consultants. This inertia can and does kill analytic cultures.

We leave this chapter with three points to take note (1) personnel attrition, by itself, will kill an analytics culture when process is absent, (2) regularly measure the efficiency and effectiveness of processes, and (3) governance done right is not long, hard, or expensive – it is just disciplined.

7 SYSTEMS

The price of light is less than the cost of darkness – Arthur C. Nielsen[1]

BigCo, Inc. buys the greatest analytics tool on the planet and hires Danny Data, the greatest Data Scientist in this quadrant of the galaxy. Jimmy, the best CEO BigCo has ever had, calls Danny to ask, "Will we make our revenue target this quarter?". Danny says he'll get back after he does his analysis. Some days later, Danny calls Jimmy and responds, "Sure as shootn' Jimmy, we'll make those dang numbers!".

Given that BigCo has the best CEO, Data Scientist, and analytic tool, has BigCo created a culture of data driven decisions? No! All they have is a man with a tool that the CEO can ask ad-hoc questions of, but no culture of data driven decisions with analytics.

Systems are the enablers of the culture of data driven decisions and, the hub of a data driven decision culture. But a tool, by itself, is not a culture.

A tool can also be the "wrong" tool. Now, wrong does not mean bad. It means a mismatch between the Personas or user's capabilities. The latter of which is one of the two main causes to system failure; i.e. *when the tool's usability exceeds the user's capacity to learn the tool in a period of time acceptable to the user.*

For example, if a user is willing to dedicate a week in training to learn a tool and a week of use to be proficient, but the tool requires a month of use, then the user will abandon the tool after a week.

The other great cause of failure is when management does not enable users with the time to learn the tool. Users are sent to training but, management fails to allot subsequent time after training for the user to become competent. The tool is thereafter abandoned.

Finance cannot become a predictive powerhouse without investing in analytics software. This is the third most frequent cause of failure in developing an analytics culture; i.e. when budget will not be spent on analytics systems. Like the quote above, the price of darkness is costly, as what you do not know can and will come back to work against you.

In the journey of moving from a Reporter to a Commentator, Finance grows from simply reporting data to analysis of data. To have sufficient time as a Commentator to analyze data, Finance need be efficient delivering reports.

Efficiency means data capture and loading for regular reporting is automated. Production of regular reports also must be automated. IT or a consultant may be needed to automate data gathering combined with BI and/or Data & Visualization (DV) tools to automate the production of reports.

Effective reporting is that which is needed to support decision making. To get there means Finance and the business must collaborate to identify such reports and assure the tools used can deliver the needed information.

In advancing towards the Advisor, Finance delivers deeper information and insight. Insight is defined as information that tells the business something that it does not know. To do so, Desktop Statistical and/or Discovery, Visualization & Analytic (DVA) tools are used.

In the final step of moving to the Strategist, Finance predicts the future and simulates potential outcomes. To a limited extent, Desktop Stat (using techniques as smoothing to forecast at high level) can also be used. But to be able to go all the way and do detail level data mining and Monte Carlo simulations with big data and Artificial

Intelligence will require Discovery, Visualization & Analytic (DVA) tools.

Figure 7-1 below reviews the Analytics System Roadmap associating Mindset, Personas and Systems. To move beyond a Reporter, Finance must provide employees with the right systems. It is important that the Mindset and investments in technologies are aligned. A Reporter Mindset with a DVA tool doesn't add value nor does a Strategist Mindset who only has access to Excel. Neither example has the capabilities to achieve a culture of analytics decisions.

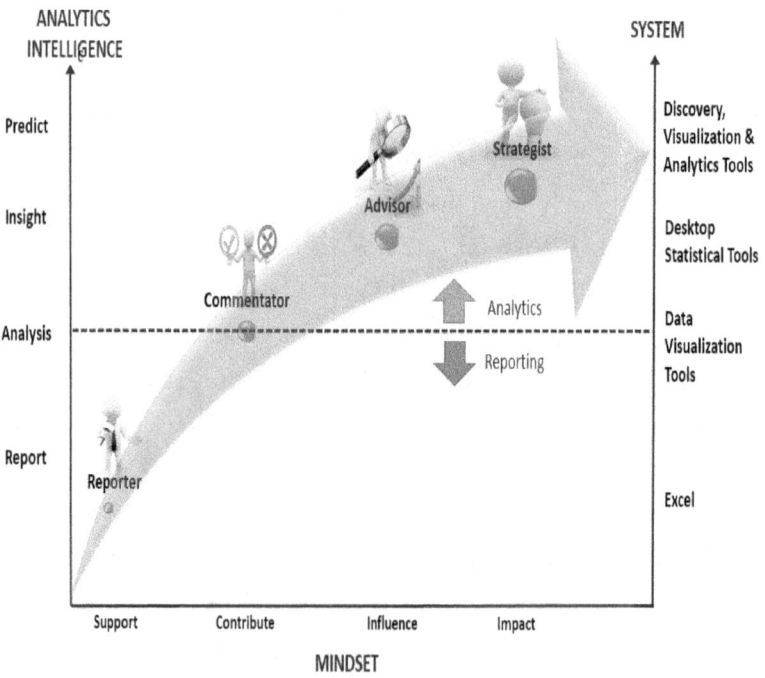

Figure 7-1: Analytics System Roadmap

The Toxic Productivity Landscape

Today, spreadsheets are the uber technology in Finance and Operations for reporting, analytics, and planning. We all have used Excel for so long we think we were born knowing it. But at one time we had to learn it and, if you can remember that far back, it was not easy. But now that we know Excel, the level of effort seems too high to learn anything else.

In many ways, it is like learning a new language. "Why bother learning Danish when I can speak English and communicate with everybody else."

So often when Finance is asked for a report or analysis the response is "I can do that (in a spreadsheet) in a few minutes". But how long does it really take? Well sometimes a few minutes and sometimes a few hours but that's only the first part of the story.

Often the reports are reused and then there is the regular maintenance of data gathering and compiling the report, all of which is very time consuming. Then if the spreadsheet is of any size, there are lurking errors. Most any survey done by the major consulting firms puts the probability of a data, security, or logic error in spreadsheets at between 90% to 100%!

Even for those many reports that are one-time, the attitude of "I can do that in a minute" comes back to kill productivity. As ad-hoc requests and routine work accumulates so the day becomes full. Ten requests for one-minute reports, actually take 10 to 20 minutes each and consumes the morning before any other work begins.

Now, the claim that ad-hoc reporting is part of the job is true and, especially, when there is no self-service user inquiry tool. However, this is and should be a minority of instances.

It is more often that the Finance "one-minute" attitude combined with business user's laziness to learn a self-service tool fuses to form a toxic mix to kill Finance's productivity. This is the landscape of most Finance groups and is the central inhibitor to advancing beyond the Reporter Persona.

A Primer on Technologies

The Table 7-1 below provides an overview of systems for Finance. Excel needs no discussion other than it is overused. Not mentioned in the Table is Python and R as these should not be confused with systems. Python is a computer language for analytics and R (or technically the R Foundation) is a library of open source formulas.

Also, not mentioned in the Table are enterprise data mining tools (e.g. SAS and SPSS). These tools are very large, complicated, expensive, and required mathematical and programming knowledge that is too often beyond the skill sets and budgets of most Finance organizations.

System Type	Distinction	Data Set	Mindset Persona
Excel	High level, custom, fraught with errors	Small	Reporter
Data Visualization (DV)	Comprehensive dashboard to visualize trends for insights	Large/ Multi Source	Commentator & Advisor
Desktop Statistical (DS)	Statistical add-on applications to Excel	Small	Advisor
Discovery, Visualization & Analytic (DVA)	Insights & foresight to find undetected opportunities & risks	Large/ Multi Source	Advisor & Strategist
Artificial Intelligence (AI)	Machine decisions that make predictions	Large/ Multi Source	Strategist

Table 7-1: Systems Landscape

DV tools provide visualization of trends and are most useful in understanding past performance. However, visualization tools are often not predictive and can lead to false negatives and positives. Further, people get wrapped-up in "beautiful" visualization pictures without much thought of how these pictures lead to better decisions.

DS tools enable statistical analysis on small data sets. They are cheap (often Excel add-ons) and ready to go out of the box. However, you will need statistical skill to take advantage of their capabilities and, because they are data limited, they will not serve a big data or enterprise environment.

Many DVA tools come with AI and statistical analysis. Machine Learning (ML) is one type of AI as is neural nets, Systematic Intelligence™ and many other forms. AI is broadly defined as a machine making human decisions.

From Excel to DVA the amount of data and the number of sources of data increases dramatically. A DVA tool will contain trillions of cells of data and analysis. This is far beyond the comprehension and capacity of humans and spreadsheets.

To make the point, one trillion cells of data is equivalent to 10,000 spreadsheets that are 100 columns wide and 1 million lines deep. And this is just the data and calculated data. It does not include reports, charts, or dashboards.

What's the Delay with Analytics?

In our survey (and those of others) some 90% of Finance groups say they want to incorporate analytics for data driven decisions. Yet, according to our survey on Figure 7-2 below only about a third are meaningfully engaged when considering tools other than Excel.

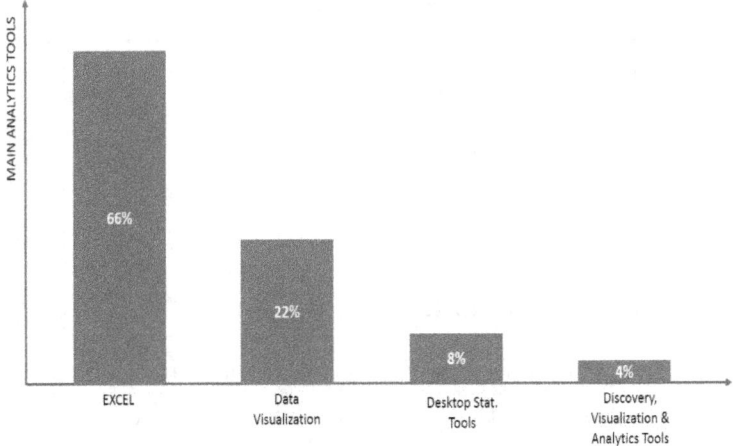

Figure 7-2: Analytics Engagement

The big hold-up is presented on Figure 7-3 below that shows 75% of Finance time consumed with spreadsheets and over 60% saying they have no time available to improve FP&A. This is not the issue for the Reporter Persona but, without automation of reporting and incorporation of tools needed to do big data analytics, there is simply no pathway toward a culture of data driven decisions.

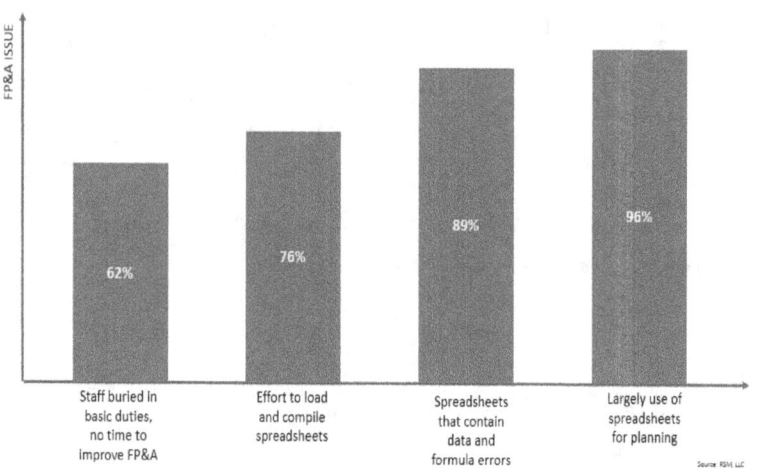

Figure 7-3: FP&A Issues

Reporter & Commentator Systems

The Reporter persona does not worry about efficiency or effectiveness of reporting, just delivering those reports accurately and timely to those who are to get the reports. This is the basics of financial reporting and all Finance groups do this, often using a combination of BI and spreadsheets. However, as these tools are limited and inflexible, there is just so much that can be accomplished. Accordingly, victory is a low bar.

The next step of the Commentator starts with the incorporation of Data Visualization (DV) tools to both make regular reporting more efficient and effective. Here, less time and headcount are needed to compose regular reports, which frees time to make more effective reporting from data analysis. Better use of BI and incorporation of DV is the first step in the automation of regular reporting and to eliminate most of the spreadsheet reports.

One key item to tackle is getting users to buy-in that reporting is better automated and that the "form" of the report should not trump substance. Most often Finance claims that report formats cannot be changed. When asked why, the often-heard response is that the user "wants it that way".

If the same data is being given in a different format, it is simply laziness for not accepting the new format. Users should be told that the company should not bear unnecessary expenses for burning personnel time to create reports that have no added value and are costly to assemble.

For example, in a multi-billion-dollar healthcare company, Finance had to manually assemble a packet of some two dozen reports derived from spreadsheets that took a team of five in FP&A a week to assemble. This could be automated in a DV tool, however, one of the reports would be presented vertically vs. horizontally, and another report would have slightly different but more complete and better information.

The idea was rejected because "that's not the way the users are accustom to getting the reports". Form supplanted substance and valuable FP&A time was spent on manually preparing reports. To add insult to injury, as the company grew, the solution was not to automate but to . . . add more headcount to prepare spreadsheet reports!

Once we embrace report automation, engaging DV tools can offer information through trend visualization and multi-dimensional comparisons.

For example, the typical year-over-year spreadsheet report on Figure 7-4 below is informative, but it's like looking into the business through a pinhole. Net Sales are up 6.8% compared to last year but is this good? With nothing more to go by, we'll all say yes.

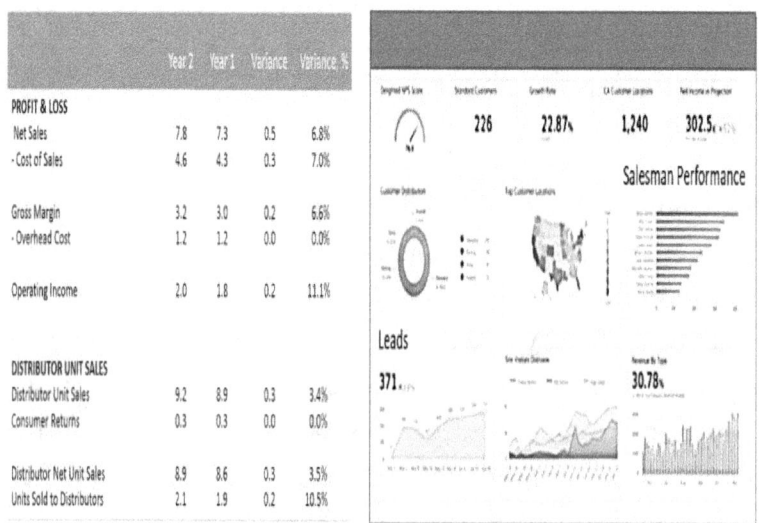

Figure 7-4: Report vs. Visualization[2]

However, the visualized dashboard on Figure 7-4 tells more. First, the graph of Leads in the lower left-hand corner shows the trend of leads have reached a plateau. Second, the middle chart on the right-hand side that measures Salesmen Performance depicts a wide variation. Thus, sales growth is at risk of slowing or declining from slowing sales leads or if one of the two top salesmen quit.

Visualization can shine a spotlight into the data that spreadsheets cannot. While tabular reporting is a necessity, by itself, leaves unanswered many questions needed to make decisions that will optimize business performance.

DV tools can add better information for better decisions through visualization and, by consolidating large data from multiple sources, enables a wide range of comparisons. Further, modern cloud based DV tools are a big advance over rigid legacy BI. Users can gain a level of control and intelligence in these new tools vs. reliance on IT and inflexible Cube technology. However, there are a few points to beware with DV.

DV is not predictive thus, false negatives and positives can result. For example, on the left chart on Figure 7-5 below, what decision would you make if you thought the future of the trend would be up? Down?

From just the visualization, we would be lulled into believing the trend will continue its climb. However, the chart to the right on Figure 7-5 shows that the next month the trend went down. These are the types of misleading decisions that can result from historical visualization of the trend.

However, of interest, is that a DVA tool using a Statistical Process Control Index, would have predicted the upcoming downward reversal in January. This is an excellent example of the power of prediction to enable better decisions.

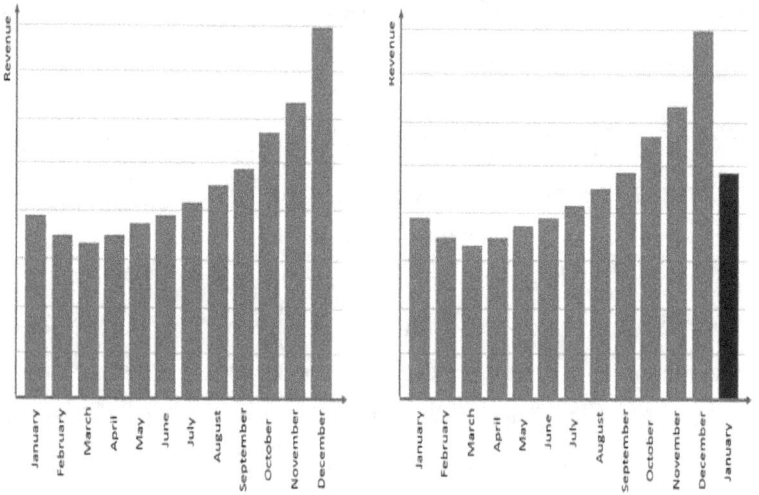

Figure 7-5: Visualization is Not Predictive

Advisors & Strategists Systems

Desktop Statistical and DVA tools can delivery powerful value through forecasting and predictions. Further, DVA tools can handle big data from many sources making analytics through whole sections of business possible.

Often, Finance wants to engage analytics but doesn't exactly know what analytics can do. As such, here is a sampling of but a small fraction of the applications of analytics:

- Predicted trend direction for better decisions
- Correlations to find disconnections with ordering
- Correlations to find the leading indicators of demand
- Long range forecasting of demand to better capex planning
- Pattern recognition to predict pipeline sales & customer churn
- Product lifecycle analysis to time promotions to optimize profit
- Monte Carlo simulation for dynamic min/max inventory optimization

Desktop Statistical tools are good to test theories, but they have limited data and dimensional capacity and need statistical knowledge for use. These tools are typically used by the Advisor for high level forecasting, small Monte Carlo simulations, correlation and other statistical analysis.

The highest ROI will be found in the DVA tools that give deep and broad insights. Most of these tools require statistical knowledge and programming, especially, when using Machine Learning (ML) that will require model training. Also, the output from DVA tools can be complex and require a translation for the business user to understand.

However, the power of DVA tools can be highlighted in a project with a Fortune 500 company. The goal was to be able to predict which sales accounts had a better propensity of closing in the current quarter.

Finance, simply using spreadsheets and exponential smoothing, was very good at forecasting the quarterly sales number. However, when confronted by the Sales group, Finance could not say which deals will likely close and those that likely will not.

To answer Sales, Finance employed a DVA tool. Taking data from the revenue and CRM systems, the tool was able to recognize patterns in the data that lead to higher and lower propensity for a deal to close in a quarter. Therefore, Finance could identify to Sales the better allocation of resources to deals that had a higher propensity to close. This foresight would maximize the sales pipeline closure rate for the quarter.

Best Practices & Benchmarks for Systems

There are a few key best practices when implementing analytic tools. This is nowhere near a complete list, just several important stepping stones that are as much what not to do as to do.

Best Practices

- Persona and System alignment: if the goal of Finance is a Strategist Persona, then DVA tools will be the bill-of-fare. If Excel is the tool, then it is an exercise in futility.

- Data Governance is part of your job - not IT: as discussed in Section 6, Process, data governance is not a full-time job. It is part of the work that is distributed across Finance and the business. Relying on IT will doom data governance to be minimally effective at best.

- Data cleaning comes from data use vs. an IT project: if you hear IT claim the need for a data cleansing project before analytics can begin, throw them out of the room! Data cleaning is a result of using data, as that use exposes the data that's "bad". As previously mentioned, the saying garbage-in-garbage-out while true, ignores that finding the garbage is a result of using it.

- Finance owns analytics - not IT: the kiss of death for implementing analytics is having IT lead or decide the selection of the analytics tool. It's Finance's tool that *only* Finance can evaluate. Consultants or IT can be used to define a selection "process" but these people should *not* have a say in selection or even in the identification of prospective vendors as these sources are fraught with prejudices. It's up to Finance to identify, specify, evaluate, and finally decide.

- System selection is hands-on: the best way to know if a system will work for you is for you to be hands-on with the software. To load your data, build a model, and analyze, predict, chart and forecast. Vendor references are fine, having a demo your data in their system is better, but using the software for a day is the "acid-test" of usability, accuracy, and ability to produce value.

Benchmarks

Successful implementation of data driven decisions with the appropriate analytics tool and attainment of the Commentator Persona and beyond, should have the following key benchmarks, *at a minimum*:

1. Regular reporting automated with little to no manual effort
2. 80% of ad-hoc inquires delivered by self-service tools
3. 50% of Finance time spent on visualization & analytics
4. 50% reduction in time to complete budgets
5. 50% reduction in forecast/budget errors
6. Strategy connected to operations

Conclusion

Analytical systems are the "hub" of data driven decisions. Select them well, use them effectively, and by every survey of every major consulting firm the ROI is at least 10:1. Finance, at a minimum, should elevate to the Commentator. Beyond that, per Figure 7-6 below, it must employ People with the characteristics and skills for the advanced Personas and equip them with the requisite Toolbox.

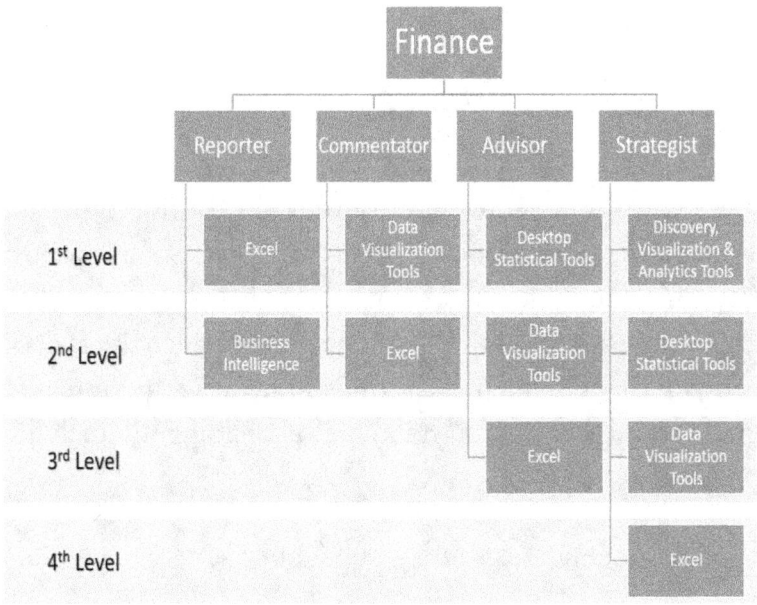

Figure 7-6: Finance Toolbox

8 BENCHMARKING

An ounce of performance is worth pounds of promises – Mae West[1]

We have now covered the journey on the Roadmap to implementing analytics. The chapters that follow introduce activities that optimize the culture of data driven decisions. In this chapter, we introduce the task of benchmarking, which establishes baselines and targets to measure the evolution and value of building an analytics culture.

Regular benchmarking measures how effective the performance improvements are over time. It contributes to the definition of the improvement strategy, by identifying where operations lead and lag vs. competition, whether that competition is internal or external.

Traditional Finance benchmarking focuses on the ratio of

Finance cost related to company revenue. The actions for Finance have been around efficiencies and how to reduce this ratio. For Next Generation Finance, the benchmark should be expanded to how much value Finance can create to make better decisions that drive the top-line.

When developing the benchmarks keep in mind that according to research[2] the top challenges to unlock the power of data and analytics to drive decision making are technology, budget, security, skills, and data management.

Benchmark Framework

Benchmarking should be implemented as a structured, systematic, and continuous process. It will not be successful if applied in an ad-hoc fashion or random basis. In most cases benchmarking is a best-practice that is part of a continuous improvement program that incorporates a feedback loop.

Benchmarking starts by understanding what is important to the company and measures performance against these factors. The gap between actual performance and preferred achievement is analyzed and an implementation plan for how to close the gap is launched. Finally, the achieved status is evaluated, a new benchmark is defined, and the next iteration is begun.

Benchmarking is a cycle of self-evaluation involving four phases as presented on Figure 8-1 below.

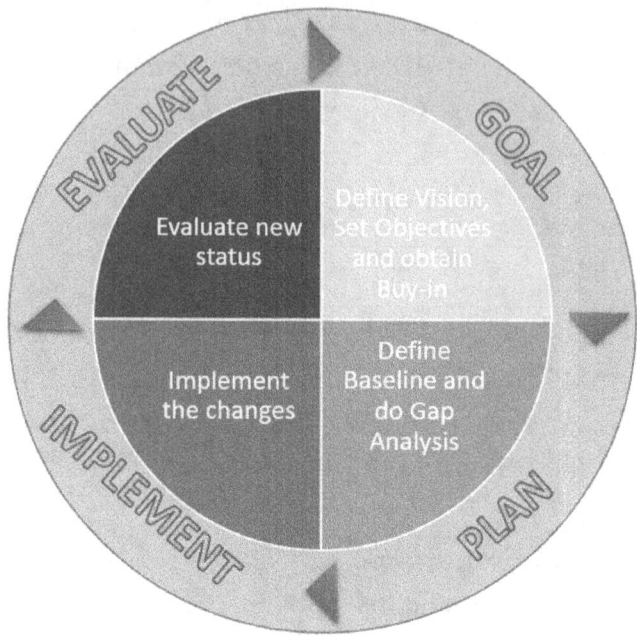

Figure 8-1: Benchmark Framework

Benchmarking covers (1) setting the **Goal** for the future, (2) defining the **Plan** including a baseline analysis and gap analysis, (3) **Implement** the Plan for how to close the gap to achieve the Goal, and (4) **Evaluate** the outcome and redefine new objectives and iterate. Benchmarking is a regular process for advancement.

1. Goal

The Goal is what benefits are to be achieved and that can be measured. For example, external benchmarks are most often found around Finance expenses as a ratio of total company revenue as compared to other companies/competitors. Finance expense ratio to revenue, according to studies[3] is around 0.6% for the median, and 0.9% for the top quartile. Of course, company size, industry, geography, etc. all affects the ratio.

The important goal for Next Generation Finance is to understand how time is spent between data gathering/reporting on one end of the Mindset and analytical insight/foresight on the other end. The other important element when setting the goal, is the systems available such as Excel/BI to advanced Desktop Statistical and Discovery, Visualization and Analytics Tools.

To achieve a real competitive advantage, Finance needs new and innovative thinking together with a willingness to explore new technologies and ways of working. The leading Finance organizations spend less on general accounting, financial reporting, and traditional transactional processes, and more on value added analytics.

A. Vision

Vision is an aspirational description of what you would like to achieve or accomplish in the mid-term or long-term future. It is intended to serve as a clear self-motivating guide for choosing current and future courses of action. For example, becoming a Strategic partner to impact business decisions though data driven decisions from analytics.

B. Objectives

The objectives are the elements Finance wants to change to achieve the vision and to move from one Mindset to the next. We suggest objectives utilize the **SMART** principle.

- **S**pecific: What do you want to achieve?
- **M**easurable: How will you know when you have reached it?
- **A**chievable: What steps will you take to achieve it?
- **R**ealistic: Can you realistically achieve it?
- **T**imely: When is the due date it should be achieved?

Specific objectives are set using the framework of Reporter, Commentator, Advisor, and Strategist. In this way the objectives can be clearly defined to be **Measurable** and Finance understands exactly which steps to take to **Achieve** the goal. Objectives need to be **Realistic** and aligned with the aspiration of Finance with a defined **Time** for when a goal is to be accomplished.

Fundamental objectives to consider for Next Generation Finance are time spent on general accounting, data capturing, financial reporting, and traditional transactional processes. These objectives are the specifics that need to be improved by the Commentator to free time for visualization and analysis. To attain analytics for insight and foresight by the Advisor and Strategist, respectively, Next Generation Finance need consider the advancement to tools beyond Excel and the skills of the people to utilize these tools to do data analysis and communicate the results in a form and format that is digestible by the business to make data driven decisions.

C. Buy-In

Buy-in to the concept of implementing analytics for data driven decisions are required to assure all levels in Finance have the same aspiration. It is also important that Finance assures the business has the appetite for Next Generation Finance.

2. Plan

The plan starts with generating the baseline for the current performance, then a Gap analysis bridging the current state with the future vision/goal, and then a plan for how to get from the identified baseline to the desired goal.

A. Baseline

The understanding of where Finance is today is the baseline for the benchmark. This step involves collecting data to define the current stage; e.g. questionnaires, interviews, shadowing another Finance organization, etc. When setting the baseline, it is important to identify the best sources of information, as well as, the best people to involve to provide the data. In the baseline analysis Finance determines if it is a Reporter, Commentator, Advisor, or Strategist.

B. Gap Analysis

Upon finishing the baseline, you should have complete, accurate, and relevant data that can be compared to either internal or external benchmarks. Internal benchmarks are used if the goal is to get to the level of other Finance organizations in the company. External benchmarks are used if your goal is to be comparable with Finance organizations of other companies.

Gap analysis against internal benchmarks is used for the Reporter or Commentator as they want to advance to the next level. Through internal benchmarking Finance can gather information from peers in the organization for how to become more efficient doing reporting and simple analysis (move from Reporter to Commentator).

Gap analysis against external benchmarks are also relevant for the Reporter and Commentator. External benchmarks are often found from research provided by the consultant companies (like ratios for finance expenses to company revenue or time spent on analytics vs. data gathering).

Gap analysis for the Advisor and Strategist are often done against external benchmarking (as there are usually no internal peers who found the Holy Grail to advanced analytics).

However, best in class external Finance organizations may not be available within your network of external companies.

Alternatively, a benchmark may be found through Thought Leader Round Tables or attending interactive Advanced Academies where external peers share their experience.

The best external benchmark is obtained by engaging an organization/institute, who has an extensive database that can provide an independent benchmark of your Finance organization against the Finance community

at different levels like job title, region, size, and industry[4].

The correct implementation of this step will result in a clear picture of your current situation in comparison with other internal or external Finance organizations. The incorrect implementation will result in imprecise information that will not be useful for improving your Finance organization.

3. Implement

When the baseline has been set, gap analysis performed, and the plan defined, Finance is ready to implement its plan.

Implementing involves understanding how to mature from one Mindset to another and what it takes from both analytical and technology skills and systems. Without aligning Mindset and Systems, Finance cannot mature from its current stage.

From Reporter to Commentator

To advance to the Commentator, Finance has to limit the use of large and many Excel files by improving reporting efficiencies by utilizing Data Visualizations tools. The Commentator also talks to business leaders to understand the reports that are needed and reports not being used. The Commentator does not run unnecessary reports, as he is in constant in dialogue with the business. Improved reporting efficiencies allow more time on simple analysis like trend visualization, detailed variance analysis, efficiency analysis, KPI measurement, etc.

From Commentator to Advisor

To become an Advisor, the focus shifts from analyzing hindsight information to analytics that generate insights to influence decisions. The Advisor uses Desktop Statistical tools for simple analytics on small data sets and Discovery, Visualization & Analytic tools for more sophisticated analysis on large and diverse data sets.

Analytics come with recommendations for how the business can adjust and improve operations. The insight provided is deeper information that will explain what and where things happen, as well as, why things happen.

The Advisor is using data to tell the business something they are not aware of; e.g. correlations between customer satisfaction and revenue. The Advisor uses that insight to generate sensitivity analysis for the business to understand how much an additional percent improvement of customer satisfaction will influence revenue.

From Advisor to Strategist

Finance operating as the Strategist has a developed analytical skillset and able to think out of the box. Finance has access to advanced tools including Discovery, Visualization & Analytics that enables Finance to provide detailed foresight.

The Strategist predicts events and provides foresight about what might happen and how to make it happen. From using simple predictive techniques like smoothing and regression, Finance can explain what might happen. As the Strategist matures, he focuses on how to make things happen from big data analytics utilizing advanced analytical tools with Artificial Intelligence capabilities.

4. Evaluate

After a period of time, Finance measures the outcomes to determine if the goals have been achieved, and what effect the changes have had. If the gap to the benchmark has not been achieved in the defined timeline then the time can be extended. Remember benchmarking is a continuous process so if the goal has been achieved a new goals defined, and a new cycle begun.

Conclusion

Benchmarks are not burdensome when executed with discipline and the requisite skills and analytical capabilities. Consultants can be useful resources to support benchmarking but, only when used to supplement Finance resources and *not* to control the process or replace Finance to perform the benchmark.

Finance often think they are at a much higher baseline than what the baseline results often reveal. For some Finance organizations benchmarking is often a hurdle. Usually, Finance simply does not want to invest the time and capital in benchmarking. However, benchmarking is a continuous process. The "heavy lifting" is in the first cycle, with each iteration becoming easier as the process is better known.

There are several challenges to be aware of when starting a benchmark project including getting reliable data, finding the best benchmarks, push back from the business, budget for analytic tools, and a lack of desire to change from the current state. However, for Finance to secure the optimization of the implementation of an analytics culture it will need to engage benchmarking as a continuous process.

Periodically, in 6-, 12- or 18-month intervals, an Analytics Culture Roadmap Survey should be performed. This is a Benchmark to assess the current state of Finance

(Reporter, Commentator, Advisor or Strategist) as compared to a previous assessment and current state of the Finance Community. Often Finance involves a third party consultant or Institute to perform and track the Roadmap progression[4].

9 STORYTELLING

Storytelling is the essential human activity. The harder the situation, the more essential it is – Tim O'Brien[1]

When a culture of data driven decisions is established with the Mindset, People, Processes, and Systems aligned and institutionalized, business growth becomes a plan and not a chance of the market. To enhance the effectiveness of decisions with analytics, we now explore the skill of storytelling with analytics to help decision makers make effective decisions.

The adage that the "A" student in college becomes the top researcher of the company, the "B" student runs the research lab, and the "C" student owns the company has much empirical support. So, for all the C students that own their companies or fill the executive ranks, storytelling needs to be developed to enable these folks to better digest and use analytics in their decision process.

This looks funny, as it is meant to, but there is a vein of truth. Witness how executives become enamored with "shinny" objects. They cause their business to buy a system because it has pretty dashboards. Or they ignore a finding from an analytic tool because they do not understand the analytics chart. Or, they simply don't believe the analytics or predictions.

For example, once upon a time, there was a major regional grocer who had in-store bakeries. The grocer was growing rapidly, and even faster was the growth of sales in the bakeries.

Our Hero (an Analytics Expert) arrived at the behest of the CFO who "felt" something was not right but could not quantify it. Our Hero did some impressive analytics that was presented to the CEO. Our Hero told the big-man that for every $1 of bakery sales there was $1.15 of total cost, with the prediction that sales growth would stop within the next year and the grocer would be in a serious cash-flow bind.

The CEO jumped from his seat and returned minutes later with a stack of papers and a calculator. Feverishly, for the next 5 minutes, he flipped pages and punched numbers. Then the CEO looked-up at the table to make his pronouncement – Bull!

With the patients of a saint, our Hero explained his analytics to the CEO. The CFO, sitting next to our Hero, was shaking his head north and south in agreement. Our Hero continued to explain how growth was masking many underlying inefficiencies. The CEO politely listened then thanked all for their time as he showed them the door.

So, what happened? The essence was that our Hero "explained" the results; i.e. he was quantitatively accurate but not "engaging" the mind of the CEO. You see, explanations are for the analytically inclined and the CEO was not analytical. Our Hero failed to tell a story. The absorption of stories is inbred in humans and we have used stories throughout the ages. Stories engage all audiences.

The Art of the Story

Stories have a beginning, middle and end. You cannot just present the end; i.e. the conclusion. And, engaging stories are simple. Hero, villain, damsel in distress, happy ending. These are your four components to delivering analytics from which decisions can be made.

Remember too, when you read books and magazines, you are drawn to pictures. You'll stare at a picture but race through the words.

Let's conjure an example. Jack, VP of Sales, bursts into the CEO Billy's office to say, "Great news Billy, we're hitting sales out of the park and will do it again this quarter." Billy responds, "Great news but let me check with CFO Bobby."

Bobby tells Billy that Jack is right, that year to date sales are up 12%, but Bobby's also forecast for this quarter's sales shows missing target and the future trend of revenue is predicted to be downward.

Billy calls both men into his office and asks what's going on. Jack proclaims his sales guys are on top of sales and the CRM (the collection of all salesmen forecast assessments) shows making targets.

CEO Billy then asks CFO Bobby to identify the deals that are not going to close as VP Sales Jack's guys have all deals laid out in the CRM system. With that, our intrepid CFO Bobby begins his story.

> Bobby: Jack, once upon a time, [it's always good to start with this phrase] we had one customer. Now we have many customers over many years. And during this time characteristics have developed in selling. Would you agree Jack?

> Jack: Well I can't say I can tell you what the characteristics are but that sounds reasonable.

> Bobby: What we have done is collect data over the

years from the CRM and Revenue systems. And by culling through trillions of cells of data we found a pattern. Customers that have a propensity to buy from us in any quarter show the following:

i. Their sales are up year over year
ii. They have purchased from us in the last 7 months
iii. They have a statistical purchasing index that is positive
iv. They have progressed in the pipeline to what you call a 50% risk
v. They have achieved a 90-day moving average of risk of at least 25%
vi. They have a been in pipeline with a duration of 60 days for each $100,000
vii. They have not been in the pipeline over 100 days for each $100,000

You see, Jack, all these parameters in our history of selling combine to show a customer that both want to buy from us **and** that we are actively and effectively selling to.

Now let me show you a trend chart where you can both see the past trend plus the statistical prediction of the future of the trend. (Bobby presents the chart to Billy)

Does this sound and look reasonable?

Jack: Why yes Bobby but you still have not told me which deals my sales guys have wrong in their forecast.

Bobby: Why here Jack is a report of all your sales prospects, by deal, that meet 6 to 7 of the criteria I just mentioned, meaning they have a good propensity to close this quarter. Then these are the prospects that meet 2 or less of the criteria, thus having little propensity to close. Finally, we have the deals that meet 3 to 5 of the criteria that are on the cusp and could drop either way.

So even if we close all the deals, except those meeting 2 or less criteria, we come-up short of our target this quarter. To make the quarter we have to close all the deals including those that history tells us have little to no propensity to close.

Jack, I suggest we focus our energies on those deals on the cusp, with 3 to 5 of the criteria, which will be the best deployment of your sales resources to maximize the quarter's sales.

And so, Jack, with your resources directed to the right accounts, we'll live happily ever after! [Also, a good phrase to end the story with]

Rules & Best Practices of Storytelling

There are three key rules of engagement in storytelling:

1. <u>Know thy audience</u>: you have to know what motivates your listeners and how they best absorb information. Some people cannot stay focused for long, some cannot handle mathematics, some are looking for risks, and others opportunity. Analogies help to make a point. And, remember, intellect can be inversely proportional to title!

2. <u>Keep It Simple</u>: easy to digest visualization vs. complex or crowded tables is preferred. While the storyteller is intimately familiar with all its details, the listener is typically not. Therefore, do not use unfamiliar terms and when introducing new concepts, it is best to use visual aids.

3. <u>A good story is short, clear, and compelling</u>: more detail is not better. It bogs down the conversation and risks getting side tracked before the point can be made. Clear and concise must be married to

compelling, otherwise the story unfolds something like this old-time Vaudeville tale:

Ladies and gentlemen.
I come before you to stand behind you,
To tell you something I know nothing about.
Admission free.
Pay at the door.
Plenty of seats.
But sit on the floor.

While the above tale is clear and concise it is hardly compelling, though we hear this tale every day from our politicians!

Compelling means we are called to the recommended action. If the action is to "Pay at the door" I am not compelled to act by having to "sit on the floor".

The best practices of storytelling include:

1. A good story is simple and clear with four parts:

    a. Clear and concise summary of problem: a very short background of who, where, what, why, when and how. BUT, use the powerful method of KISS (Keep It Simple Stupid).

b. Analysis that identifies the pertinent facts – as Sgt. Joe Friday of the LAPD said in the old TV series, Dragnet, "Just the facts". Too many facts are confusing. Simply present those that are absolutely needed.

c. Evaluation of what the facts mean – shy away from statistical talk but include a few visuals to aid comprehension. For example, the fact is unemployment has been declining for the past three months and it is strongly correlated to sales. A chart that shows that as unemployment has declined that sales have gone up in direct proportion is a good visual. No need to mention the coefficient of correlation is -0.978.

d. Conclusion & Recommendation – the conclusion should be obvious. Show two, but no more than three, recommended options. Two options present a simple either-or decision that is preferred with smaller value/cost decisions. For larger decisions, three choices are better, as humans tend to shy away from the lower cost (thinking that it is cheap) but fear the higher cost (as "I can't afford") and therefore tend to the middle (Goldilocks) option.

2. A good presentation answers questions in advance of there being asked. When reviewing a

presentation ask yourself, "Does this slide provoke an unanswered question?" If yes, you need to change the content.

3. Less is more. For most storytelling the entire presentation, as a rule of thumb, should be contained to 10 to 20 minutes. The Summary is no more than 1-2 minutes, then analysis and evaluation in 8-16 minutes, and 2-4 minutes for conclusion and recommendation. Only about a dozen or so lightly filled slides, half that are visualized, are needed.

Conclusion

Storytelling is the linchpin to making the culture of data driven decisions with analytics work. When done well, decision makers will have accurate, timely, complete, and _understandable_ information and predictions from which to make better decisions.

10 SELLING THE CULTURE OF ANALYTICS

You don't have to burn books to destroy a culture. Just get people to stop reading them – Ray Bradbury[1]

When "selling" the Culture of Analytics to Finance and the business, it is important to emphasize that Finance needs to master each Mindset Persona in moving from left to right on the horizontal axis in Figure 10-1.

Finance cannot be an Advisor or Strategist who convince business leaders to take data driven decision using advanced analytics if it cannot be a reliable Reporter that reports hindsight information in an accurate, timely and accessible manner.

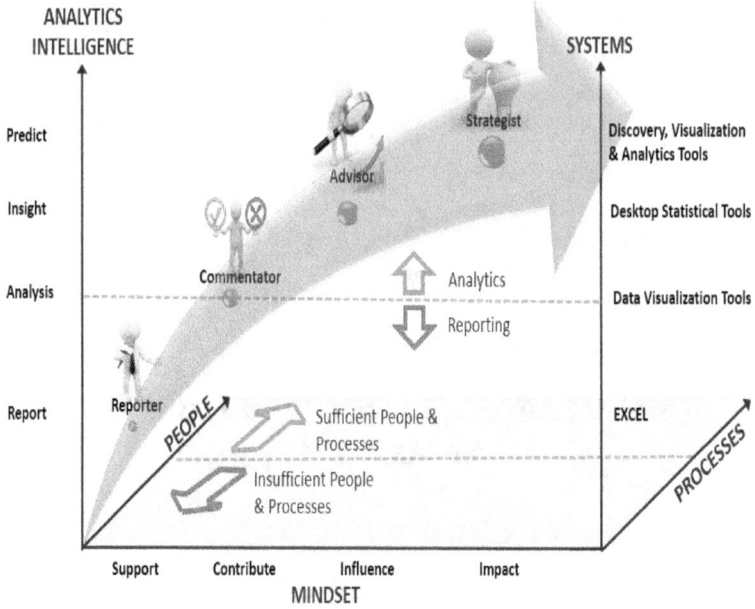

Figure 10-1: Roadmap to Analytics Culture

To build an analytics culture, Finance must understand how to move from the Reporter to a Strategist by aligning the four components of Mindset, People, Processes, and Systems. If one of the components is missed, Finance will not be able to build a culture that delivers value-add insight and foresight to influence business leaders and impact the strategic direction of the company.

Mindset is the first component in creating an analytics culture. Accordingly, Finance leaders are focused on improving skill sets for driving analytics. Then, Finance requires advanced analytics tools, as value-add insight and foresight cannot be generated from just Excel and BI.

Tools such as Desktop Statistical and Discovery, Visualization & Analytics are essential to make data driven decisions.

Finally, Finance requires sufficient People and Processes including the right people to drive advanced analytics, and documented processes to institutionalize analytics as a culture for data driven decision. Without written procedures there can be no sustainable culture, as advanced analytics will evaporate when the people who drive it leave the organization.

Selling Analytics to Finance

The word "analytics" is often misused within Finance. It is important to understand that reporting historical numbers is NOT analytics. Also rolling-up a forecast from the sales organization is NOT analytics either. Even though this "forecast" is an expression of the future, it is merely consolidating guesses without validating the data through the use of unbiased analytics tools and techniques.

The starting point of analytics is when Finance provides **better information** as a Commentator from visualization that reveals, for example, trends in a times series. From there analytics evolve **deeper information,** like insight from correlations between financial and non-financial data used to influence decisions making. The final destination for analytics is when data is used for **predictive information** and Finance impacts strategic directions from predicting future events.

There are many routes for Finance to become an analytics powerhouse but, common for all, is the Roadmap in Figure 10-1 above. Selling the culture of data driven decisions with analytics can be detailed in a pictorial formula on Figure 10-2.

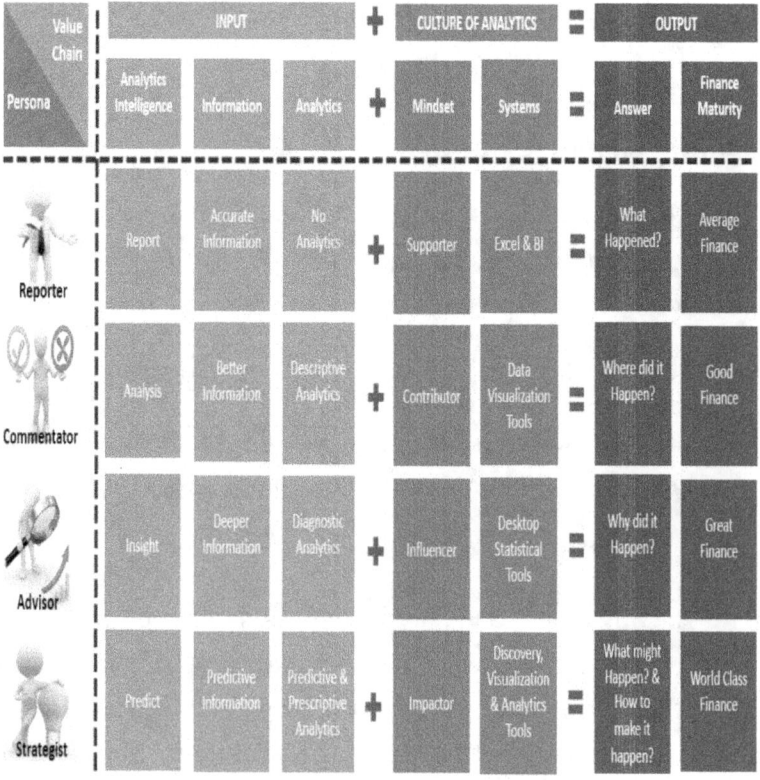

Figure 10-2: Analytics Value Chain Formula

For example, if the **Output** is to become **World Class Finance** being able to answer questions like **What might happen** and **How to make it happen,** it is important to recognize what is your Input and Analytics Culture. As such, the Strategist **Predict** by providing foresight from **Predictive information** using **Predictive and Prescriptive Analytics** techniques as **Input**. In addition, to achieve the **Culture of Analytics**, the Strategist has a Mindset of an **Impactor** who wants the business to take data driven decisions based on advanced analytics created from utilizing analytics system, like a **Discovery, Visualization and Analytics tool**.

Further, analytics is the special ingredient for both job security and satisfaction. When Finance is valued by the business, it's the Finance people that are valued. Emailing a report to a business owner that responds to his question, promotes a person's worth of his contribution. But when a high IQ guy compiles a report by copy/paste from transactional systems to spreadsheets, it is a waste of his capacity and talent.

Rather, the high IQ folk in Finance are better disposed by personal worth, job security, and job satisfaction to be proactive to analyze data in the detail that can uncover unseen opportunities and identify unknown risks. This empowers the business to make better decisions that improve performance. This is how Finance "sells" to Finance the importance of implementing analytics.

Selling Finance Analytics to the Business

Finance employees with advanced analytics skill can run head-on to the sentiment from the business that "analytics will not work" or "analytics is too complicated". At times, Finance can struggle to convince business leaders that Finance can play a more strategic role when those leaders are not up to date on the value advanced analytics can bring.

A way to move business leaders in the direction of analytics is for Finance to "plant seeds"; i.e. generate some analytical insights and keep re-visiting it with the business. As the analytical seeds start to provide insights, the business will pay attention and start to ask for more insights.

Another way to get business leaders attention, is to provide predictions about future business performance. Many Finance organization are already much better at forecasting using predictive analytics than the Sales or Marketing organizations.

When Finance demonstrate for several consecutive periods better forecasting than Sales or Marketing, then Finance will get attention from the business. As a result, the predictive analytics forecast from Finance will start to become the baseline when discussing the forecast from the Sales or Marketing organizations.

When Good Enough is Good Enough

Some businesses will simply not want Finance to provide insight and foresight to influence and impact decisions. There are lots of examples of old fashion companies where Finance is simply looked upon as the trusted scorekeeper. In these organizations, Finance will not be allowed to spend time on advancing its analytical capabilities nor invest in advanced DVA tools. As such, a Finance leader with a Strategist Persona aspiration is better to look for another company to join.

For some companies, good enough is good enough; i.e. we're profitable and growth is, well, good enough! No need to spend time and money in new-fangled stuff. This is both an attitude and strategy. But for those companies where growth is important, then good enough is a battle cry against complacency and man-the-guns to get better.

Lead or Perish

In some businesses, Finance simply follows the trail of its predecessors. However, by following tradition and, not the evolution of analytics, the future of Finance as a trusted advisor is reaching its end.

Today, too many Finance organizations focus on the surface. Finance with a Reporter Persona has already seen some of their jobs shipped to centers of excellence/shared service centers often in low cost countries. But, by finding the underlying factors that drives the business forward, Finance will secure a seat at the table as a strategic partner with the business.

It is also important to understand that if Finance doesn't take the lead of driving analytics, it could end up getting side lined. In today's world, Finance no longer has the monopoly of owning the data and access to the CEO. Data exists all over and Finance needs to take the lead and establish itself as the value-add, forward looking predictive hub. If not, other organizations are and are willing to pick up the responsibility.

The Hard Dollar Value of Analytics

Our research of public companies shows that those companies that continuously deliver reliable revenue and earnings growth are rewarded, on average, with a forward PE multiple 27% higher than the average PE multiple of a market basket of companies.

The study encompassed companies with revenue over a billion dollars in the sectors of transportation, utilities, retail, CPG, healthcare, pharma, energy, financial services, automotive, and aerospace. (The tech sector was not included as it distorts the PE profile of the other sectors). Forward PE multiples ranged from a low of 7.2 to a high of 24 with an average of 15.9. The companies with the best PE multiples across sectors averaged 20.3.

The theme of this book is better business performance through a culture of data driven decisions from analytics. Therefore, the Roadmap in Figure 10-1 to implementing a culture of analytics is also your roadmap to higher business valuation.

Analytics is the future for decision making and all decisions are about the future. Analytics drives better decisions by providing insights and foresight. Better decisions result in better planning, better resource allocation, and better business performance.

Hence, the hard dollar value for successfully implementing analytics can be translated to today's market, on average, of $4.40 of additional valuation for every dollar of earnings.

Analytics – The Undiscovered Country

Short term decisions tend to be reactionary and by the gut. Long term decisions tend to be emotional and political. Analytics help business move decisions from the qualitative "feel" to a quantitative fact-based "analysis".

The future is the brave new world of analytics. It is transformative for business operations because it is objective and comprehensive. It separates the "heat from the light" to remove the bias.

Analytics when properly incorporated into the decision

process can produce sustained and measurable improvement in revenue, earnings, and valuation that result from better planning and decisions that optimize business performance.

Conclusion & Summary

Selling the Culture of Analytics starts with Finance having a vision and aspiration to move towards world class. To implement analytics for data driven decisions Finance needs to provide analytical insight and foresight that influence business leaders and impact the strategic direction for the company.

For Finance to get there it needs to build an analytics culture that includes the four components of: Mindset, People, Process, and Systems. Further all four components for an analytics culture must be aligned and institutionalized for data driven decisions to be sustained.

The first building block in the journey of a culture for analytics is **Mindset**. Finance will get a more strategic role by delivering insight and foresight to take data driven decisions. If Finance sees its role as merely the "print shop" that delivers profit and loss reports, then they are the trusted scorekeeper, nothing more.

The second building block is **People** who can deliver advanced analytics and be collaborative with the business to enable the business to take data driven decisions. If Finance only has CPAs and Excel "jockeys", Finance will have limited ability to provide advanced analytics insight and foresight. This is not to promote that Finance needs Data Scientists, but to identify that going beyond the Reporter Persona requires People who think out-of-the-box and use advanced analytic tools and techniques.

The third building block is **Process** encompassing Data Governance and Decision Governance. Without access to reliable data and a clearly defined decision processes, the culture of analytical decision making cannot be maintained. Finance needs to document and institutionalize the processes for delivering advanced analytics to business leaders, else as the People who drive advanced analytics leave the organization the analytics culture will not die with their departure.

The fourth building block is **Systems**. With the right Mindset, People, and Processes Finance requires the right advanced analytical software for data driven decisions. Predictive and Big Data analytics is just too complex to be analyzed by humans and spreadsheets, as this combination does not have the capability nor capacity to see detailed relationships between large numbers of variables and dimensions over time. Insight and foresight require an investment in advanced DVA tools.

The "pay-off" for implementing analytics is large in Dollars, Job Security, and Job Satisfaction!

ABOUT THE AUTHOR

Robert J Zwerling, P.E.

Mr. Zwerling is a high-tech entrepreneur, founding and growing software companies in telecommunication, manufacturing & distribution, high data availability, and predictive analytics. His accomplishments span over 25 years include patent pending artificial intelligence software, author of numerous papers, requested speaker at summits on forecasting and predictive analytics for business optimization, and inventor of the concept of Systematic Intelligence™ for big data mining.

Over the past decade, he has implemented analytics in Finance in dozens of companies ranging in size from $100 million to Fortune 500 firms across a wide breadth of industries. He architected significant exits as co-founder of the ISIS Telecom Group (sold to Computer Science Corporation, NYSE: CSC) and CEO of Vision Solutions (sold to a foreign public company).

With his daughter, he co-authored the book, 'Vigilance The Price of Liberty, What you can do today to save America tomorrow', and co-authored with Jesper H Sorensen, 'Implementing an Analytics Culture for Data Driven Decisions, A Manifesto for Next Generation Finance'.

Mr. Zwerling is also involved with civics as he co-produces with US Vigilance and the Richard Nixon Foundation, *The Collegiate Forum*, which brings together bright college students from major California universities to discuss current political topics at the Richard Nixon Presidential Library. He is also a member of Stanford University's Hoover Institution.

Mr. Zwerling is currently founder and Managing Director of Aurora Predictions, a company that provides Systematic Intelligence™ with AI that is packaged with an Excel style user interface to enable Finance organizations to take control to develop insights and foresights that optimizes business performance.

He holds a Bachelor in Engineering (Magna Cum Laude) in mechanical engineering from Stony Brook University, and a Master of Science in Mechanical Engineering (majoring in thermodynamics and fluid mechanics) from CSU Los Angeles. He is a member of Tau Beta Pi Engineering Honor Society, and a licensed Professional Engineer in CA.

Jesper Hybholt Sorensen

Mr. Sorensen is a Finance Executive with a proven track record of advancing the analytics agenda. Using advanced analytics and strategic insight and foresight he influences business leaders to take data driven decisions and has been recognized for improving top line growth and profitability in large corporations.

Mr. Sorensen has been with Oracle, DuPont and IBM and he been leading global finance teams for multi-billion-dollar businesses. He holds several advisory positions including advisory board member for Aurora Predictions and analytics expert for the International Institute of Analytics.

Mr. Sorensen is a highly respected keynote speaker who has been featured at several conferences in San Francisco, San Diego, Chicago and Boston. He covers topics like Strategic Business Partnering, Next Generation Finance, and Advanced Analytics. He co-authored the book, 'Implementing an Analytics Culture for Data Driven Decisions, A Manifesto for Next Generation Finance' with Robert J Zwerling and has published several Finance articles and research papers.

He holds a Master Degree in Economics and Management from the University of Aarhus, Denmark. He is a certified Six Sigma Green Belt, and is certified in Risk Management and Strategic Decision Making from Stanford University.

APPENDIX

Appendix A – Capability Model

The table below is an example of the Capability Model discussed in Chapter 4, Mindset. This can be used as a "yardstick" to assess where a Finance group sits with respect to Next Generation Finance.

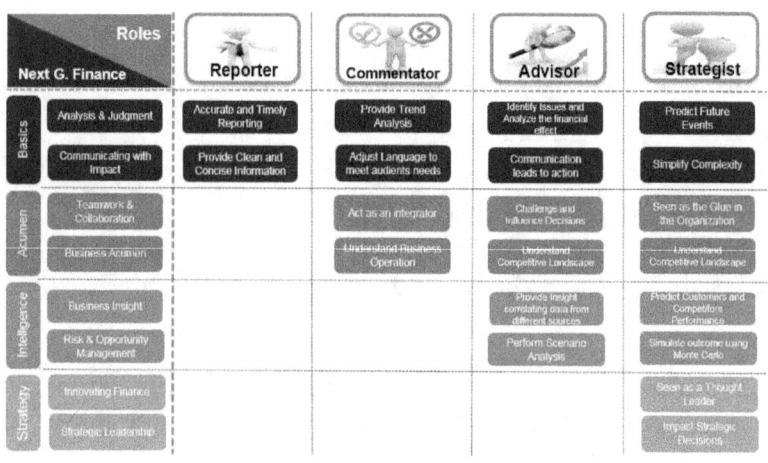

Figure A-1: Capability Matrix example

Appendix B – Sample Processes

Provided below is a sample framework for us in building processes for Data and Decision Governance.

Data Governance – Organization

For your company answers the questions below for preparing regular reports; e.g. corporate financials, rolling forecast, budget, monthly performance, etc.

- Where are the data sources?
- Who is responsible for updating the sources?
- When are the sources updated?
- How are corrections to the sources made?
- What is the data that needs to be exported and imported from/to the sources?
- When does this need to happen?

From the above, make a process flow. Figure B-1 below offers a sample.

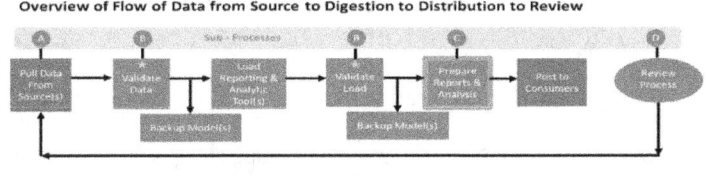

Overview of Flow of Data from Source to Digestion to Distribution to Review

☆ Indicates places for assuring data accuracy and/or completeness

● Indicates sub processes for further description

■ Process steps with Blue indicating automation

Figure B-1: Data Governance Process Flow Chart

Each sub-process needs articulation and use Table B-1 below as guidance for the procedures to build.

Sub Process	Period	Responsible	Activity
A	Daily, Weekly, Monthly, Quarterly	• Source Owners	• Pull data from & update data to sources • Pulls should be automated • Pulls have sufficient time to allow for failure
B	Daily, Weekly, Monthly, Quarterly	• Validation by analysts • Analysts feedback to Owners on accuracy	• Data is validated for accuracy
C	Daily, Weekly, Monthly, Quarterly	• Reports automated • Analysts for analytics	• Prepare reports & assure complete data • Prepare analysis & report on insights to foresights
D	Monthly, Quarterly	• Analysts & Consumers	• Assure data accurate, complete, timely & accessible • Add/Remove data – notify source owner

Table B-1: Data Governance Subprocesses

Decision Governance – Organization

For your company, answer the questions below on the analytics used to make decisions and on what; e.g. capex, headcount, budget, etc.

- What analytics are needed?
- Who needs the analytics?
- When are the analytics needed?
- How are analytics used to make the decision?
- What is the form, forum, and manner the analytics to be delivered?

From the above, make a flow process. Figure B-2 offers a sample.

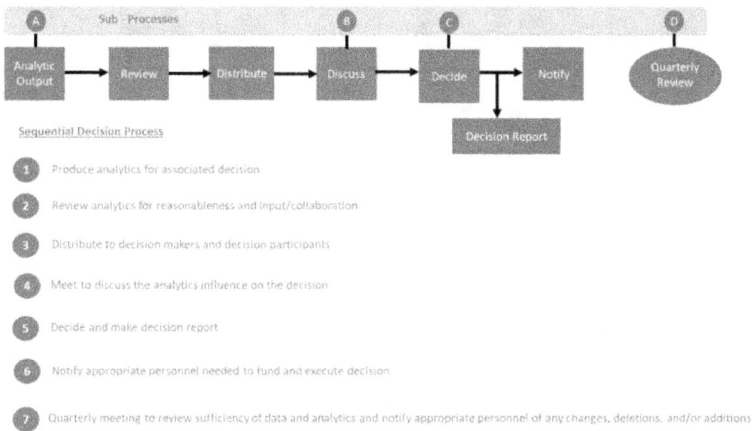

Figure B-2: Decision Governance Flowchart

Each sub-process needs articulation and use Table B-1 below as guidance for the procedures to build.

Sub Process	Period	Responsible	Activity
A	Daily, Weekly, Monthly, Quarterly	• Analysts	• Develop analytics & story
B	Daily, Weekly, Monthly, Quarterly	• Distribute & discuss meaning	• Story is told to consumers in specified form & forum
C	Daily, Weekly, Monthly, Quarterly	• Decision Makers	• Based on analytics & business feedback, Decision Makers decide
D	Monthly, Quarterly	• Analysts & Decision Makers	• Assure data & analytics accurate, complete, timely & accessible • Add/Remove analytics • Add/Remove data – notify source owner

Table B-2: Decision Governance Subprocesses

BIBLIOGRAPHY

Chapter 1 – Introduction

1. https://www.brainyquote.com/topics/insight

Chapter 2 – Next Generation Finance

1. https://www.brainyquote.com/topics/transformation
2. Deloitte: Finance Business Partnering – Less than the sum of the parts, 2014
3. PredictiCon: Next Generation Finance - From Average to World Class, 2014
4. Oracle, CIMA, CGMA: The digital finance imperative: Measure and manager what matters next, 2015
5. PWC: Finance Effectiveness Benchmark Report 2017, 2017

Chapter 3 – Roadmap

1. https://www.azquotes.com/quote/603360

Chapter 4 – Mindset

1. https://www.brainyquote.com/quotes/walt_disney_163027

Chapter 5 – People

1. https://www.forbes.com/sites/erikaandersen/2013/05/31/21-quotes-from-henry-ford-on-business-leadership-and-life/#6165e262293c
2. JPK Group Summit on Forecasting & Analytics, November 2018

Chapter 6 – Process

1. https://www.brainyquote.com/quotes/clayton_christensen_671437

Chapter 7 - Systems

1. https://quotefancy.com/quote/1761829/Arthur-Nielsen-The-price-of-light-is-less-than-the-cost-of-darkness
2. Chart from Grow, BI tool

Chapter 8 - Benchmarking

1. https://www.brainyquote.com/quotes/mae_west_164516
2. Dun & Bradstreet, Analytics Accelerates into the Mainstream, 2017
3. PWC, Finance Effectiveness Benchmark Report 2017, 2017
4. Finance Analytics Institute: http://fainstitute.com/#benchmark

Chapter 9 – Storytelling

1. https://www.brainyquote.com/quotes/tim_o
   brien_515513

Chapter 10 – Selling the Culture

1. https://www.brainyquote.com/quotes/ray_br
   adbury_120122